EMBRACING 1
FOR DISTRIBUTED
PROJECT TEAM SUCCESS

THE
VIRTUAL
EDGE

EMBRACING TECHNOLOGY
FOR DISTRIBUTED
PROJECT TEAM SUCCESS

THE
VIRTUAL
EDGE

Margery Mayer

Library of Congress Cataloging-in-Publication Data

Margery, Mayer.
    The virtual edge: embracing technology for distributed project
team success / Margery Mayer
        p.   cm.
    Includes bibliographical references (p.   ).
    ISBN: 1-880410-16-8 (pbk. : alk. paper)
    1. Groupware (Computer software)   2. Teams in the workplace-
-Computer networks.   3. Industrial project management--Computer
networks.   I. Title.
    HD66.2.M39   1998
    658.4'04'028546 – – dc21   98–6265
                                                          CIP

Published by: Project Management Institute Headquarters
            Four Campus Boulevard, Newtown Square, Pennslyvania 19073-3299 USA
            Phone: 610-356-4600 or Visit our Web Site: www.pmi.org

ISBN: 1-880410-16-8

PMI Book Team

Editor-in-Chief, James S. Pennypacker
Editor, Toni D. Knott
Proofreader, Lisa M. Fisher
Graphic Designer, Michelle T. Owen
Acquisitions Editor, Bobby R. Hensley
Production Coordinator, Mark S. Parker

PMI books are available at special quantity discounts to use as premiums and
sales promotions, or for use in corporate training programs. For more information,
please write to the Business Manager, PMI Headquarters Publishing Division, Forty
Colonial Square, Sylva, North Carolina 28779 USA. Or contact your local bookstore.

The paper used in this book complies with the Permanent Paper Standard issued by the
National Information Standards Organization (Z39.48—1984).

PMI and PMBOK are the registered trademarks of the Project Management Institute.

10   9   8   7   6   5   4   3   2   1

Acknowledgments

I would like to thank John Powers for first suggesting that I put my research into book form and for reading my first draft.

Table of Contents

Introduction

With the increasing emphasis and dependency on computer technology and network connectivity, it was only a matter of time before company executives began realizing the advantages of managing projects with a virtual project management team. Such a team consists of members who are distributed across buildings, states, and countries, who come together for a specific project and then disband when the project is completed.

Managing change is the most demonstrable feature of virtual operations, and efficient computer technology and stable networking are required to ensure success within virtual project management. While traditional project management methods embrace computer technology for project tracking and reporting, virtual project management depends upon this technology and thus cannot exist without it. The efficiency of the systems employed and the reliability of the equipment and networks are of paramount importance to a virtual corporation or virtual project management team. It may be said that traditional project management teams are composed of bricks and mortar, while the virtual team is comprised of broadband facilities, routers, and hubs. In the virtual environment, the electronic information infrastructure is no longer an overhead item to be used and depreciated; it becomes vital information and a knowledge transport system critical to success and key to gaining a competitive edge in the marketplace.

Therefore, in order to ensure a successful transition from a traditional operating corporation to a virtual corporation with virtual project teams, value and commitment must be placed on developing and supporting the electronic information infrastructure. One of the advantages to utilizing technology to such an extent is its ubiquitousness: two efforts could evolve in parallel even though occurring at different locations. This allows project team members to see the entire work effort and be able to anticipate problems and negotiate solutions while the work is still upstream, effectively eliminating costly rework.

At the same time, while the key to virtual operations is connectivity and integration, the possibilities for disintegration are a factor. Constant communication between team members is extremely important and requires access to common data, objects, and shared information, rather than data and objects having different representations in different systems. Groupware tools—tools allowing team members to dynamically communicate, respond, and update common information—are necessary in order for a virtual team and virtual project to be successful. Everyone should have the same technology, that is, a laptop computer, modem, cellular phone, voice mail, Internet access, E-mail, and pager. It goes without saying that good and reliable support is essential to the accomplishment of virtual project management; too much valuable time is lost if equipment is in need of repair, network access is impaired, or if virtual project management team members are improperly trained on the tools and equipment.

Dispersed software development teams can offer many unique advantages over traditional, co-located teams, and these virtual project teams are absolutely essential for global projects. They provide a global resource pool of talented engineers, programmers, designers, and testers and support world-class competencies. Imagine the possibilities if skilled resources were registered in a common database, regardless of company affiliation, and the project manager could quickly choose and electronically contact the very best team members from this database when a certain type of resource was needed. Such teams could raise the level of resources and the quality of the project result, reduce overall costs, eliminate major travel—and lost time while traveling—and decrease related overhead costs associated with trying to have the team and expertise located regionally.

While there are many operational similarities between traditional and virtual project management teams, significant advantages of virtual teaming center around how and where members meet and how they communicate in between times. Virtual, dispersed team members must learn how to work collaboratively with information and communication technologies while in stressful situations, with a variety of team competencies from potentially multiple locations, multiple countries, and, often, multiple companies.

Corporate politics and power plays are far less important in virtual project management when the project is the priority, thus freeing individuals to focus on their skills and contributions to the virtual project management team, with added emphasis on knowledge and capability.

All of the information in this book was researched, experienced, read, and restated based on my experience and understanding of virtual project management and distributed teams. As a consultant in process and strategy analysis, identification, recommendation, and implementation around technology in high-tech environments, I feel particularly well suited to write on the subject. If anyone is interested in determining if his corporation is ready to become virtual, or where the corporation is in terms of project management maturity prior to introducing virtual teaming, please contact me at:

Strategy and Process Experts
751 Laurel Street #550
San Carlos, California 94070
Telephone: (650) 591-4255; Fax: (650) 631-8663
E-mail: mmayer@aol.com

Margery Mayer

1

The Benefits of Collaboration

Alliances

The business world has begun to recognize the potential of the *virtual organization*, or the *virtual corporation*, as the model for corporations of the future. This type of enterprise will address the challenges of unprecedented growth and customer expectations and alternatives, global competition, time-to-market compression, complexity, rapid change, and ubiquitous technologies. In a virtual corporation model, a lead organization creates alliances, both internal and external, with a set of other groups that possess the *best in class* competencies to build specific products or services in the shortest period of time possible.

These alliances are virtual in nature because the skills required are not homogeneous to the lead organization but are hybrid groups and individuals from different corporations, including competitors, customers, and suppliers. Their purpose is not longevity but rather bringing specific, high-quality products or services to market as quickly as possible. An example might be a new pharmaceutical product that needs to be brought to market quickly to address a serious illness. Perhaps a half dozen companies join in the effort, providing stakeholders to the virtual project team with specific competencies in research and development, chemistry, physiology, marketing, testing, distribution, and support. As soon as the product is brought to market, the alliance is disbanded, and the organizations seek other teaming possibilities. The virtual project teams enhanced results and produced high-quality products and services in record time with reduced overall costs.

Teamwork

Teamwork has shaped the world, from the gathering of engineers to build a space shuttle, to winning the baseball playoffs, and even to the highly intelligent hackers who penetrate networks for the fun of it. After all, some bright engineers worked for Xerox Parc and decided to start new high-technology corporations in their garages; the result was a team effort that paid off.

In a society as complex and technologically sophisticated as ours, the most urgent projects require the coordinated contributions of the most talented people. Whether the effort is to build a global manufacturing enterprise or to discover new cures for diseases, one individual alone cannot accomplish it; a team of individuals is needed. Generally, in America, we resist the idea of team collaboration; the individual achiever syndrome—the Lone Ranger—is prevalent. We tend to underestimate just how much creativity and how many results can be generated through a team or group.

Collaboration constantly takes place whether we like it or not. Most major accomplishments have been done with the aid and assistance of others, even if one person seems to receive the credit. Teams are the natural repositories of genius; the combined effort of a few successful combinations can achieve dramatic results. It is through organizations that foster teamwork that greatness is realized, allowing participants to be better than they might be on their own. All successful teams have strong, often visionary, leaders who assist in the coordination and communication effort needed to keep the team on track. The leader often is tasked with recruiting the right mix of participants for the job; this is the first step in a good collaboration. Often these teams have dual administration, a visionary leader, and a more pragmatic person for support.

Teams tend to be nonconformist in nature as they accomplish tasks when required and often share responsibilities when necessary. The participants are never typical corporate types and are seemingly on their own tracks rather than on the corporate fast track. Like traditional project management teams, virtual teams often disband when the project is over. They are considered virtual because, unlike most traditional teams, they are often geographically dispersed in nature and come together through technology. Also, similar to traditional teams, these same resources usually become part of other project teams because they enjoy the experience, and they do their best work as members of a project team. The shared experience—to the project team member—is an essential and a rewarding learning experience.

In today's electronically borderless world, effective teaming is critical. An organization can often have a great product, the most advanced state-of-the-art hardware and software, the best talent, and the desire to work to succeed and still fall short of producing a product that fits within the schedule and cost constraints of a project. It may not have had the right team talent on the project because the local expertise could not be found when needed. Seeking expertise from wherever it is located may have assisted in bringing this product to market quicker and more efficiently. Organizations that rely on virtual project teams have the challenges of more complexities than co-located work teams because geographical diversity and the dependency on technology dramatically magnify levels of complexity.

As with traditional teams, in order for virtual teams to be effective, they must design and develop synergistic beliefs, skills, and cultural foundations. Virtual work and virtual teaming, though, depend on an extremely high level of communications and trust. Team members must learn how to work best together with information and communication technologies, with a variety of personal competencies from multiple locations, countries, and companies. In order for virtual teaming to be successful, changes in personnel, attitude, behavior, skills, and processes may be required. There is significant effort spent in coordinating the overall teaming, and it could increase dramatically if the team is not cohesive. Casual communication, body language, tonal effects, and context are often not communicated well through electronic media, and deliberate communication techniques, face to face, are more effective in some instances. The virtual project team members not only will complete the project, develop a product, or implement worldwide technologies but will learn and grow themselves as well. They will build trust, share values and vision, and as a result put forth the invested effort to help the entire organization succeed instead of merely focusing on their own pieces of the puzzle.

Corporate Examples: Xerox Corporation plants are using virtual teams in manufacturing and are 30 percent more productive than conventionally organized plants. Proctor and Gamble achieves 30 to 40 percent

Table 1. Differences Between Traditional and Virtual Project Teams

Traditional Teams	Virtual Teams
Members from the same organization	Members from organizations, companies, affiliated business partnerships, competitors
Members trained, and often certified, establishing standards	Members selected because of demonstrated competencies
Roles and expectations as per job title	Expected to perform as per skill
Little trust	Require sustained trust
Work processes rigid and defined, often not used	Work processes flexible and agreed upon by team, required for the project
Position and authority important	Knowledge and capability most important
Persuade through power	Persuade through knowledge and influence
Assert one perspective	Shared perspective; negotiate tradeoffs
Stable work environment	Environment continually changing
Minimized formal communication	Continuous structured communications, overcommunication
Members work in close proximity	Members work from distances, anywhere feasible
Hierarchical environment	Reduced hierarchy, more networked, less political

higher productivity at its eighteen virtual project team plants. This company considers virtual teams so vital to its competitive strength that it is now giving it global publicity. Shenandoah Life processes 50 percent more applications and customer service requests with 10 percent fewer people since using virtual work teams. All of these companies stopped to look at their operations and chose a more visionary approach to achieving their goals. They baselined where their companies were before changes, developed metrics for evaluating the delta changes, and were able to identify positive results from these changes.

Traditional versus Virtual Project Teams

To facilitate explaining virtual teaming, traditional teaming should be understood. Most traditional project teams are located in the same building or group of buildings, usually within a campus-type area. The teams have a leader and team members with specific functions, meet face to face on a regular basis, and stay informed by stopping by each other's desks from time to time for ad hoc communications. Project participants are visible and are easily found within the office buildings. There are exceptions to this, of course, such as in construction and field engineering projects.

A virtual or distributed project team is very different from, and yet very much the same as, a traditional project team. Both have team members, and both have project scope and expectations, but how and where members do their work is different. Neither time nor place is of much importance to a virtual team and only becomes significant at those rare times when a meeting is scheduled. Virtual project teams can be found in many areas: sports, as players change teams seasonally; business, when alliances form for specific projects; military, as troops form for specific assignments; fashion, while designers and manufacturers team for seasons; production, as expertise meets from around the globe; television, when actors, producers, and staff gather to film, paste, and edit; construction, where building expertise is hired for specific elements of a job; and news teams, who partner with others around the globe for breaking stories.

Depending on the project, usually a technology virtual team is focused on a specific project with a typical duration of six months to one year. Although often difficult to initiate and sustain, virtual teaming nonetheless offers tremendous benefits. Virtual teaming effectively deals with the realities of time and distance compression; distributed resources; increasing dependency on knowledge-based input, flexibility and adaptability; and the use of technology for communications.

Virtual teaming also enables the recruitment of the best competencies available from around the world. Experience has shown that the most effective project teams are those with diverse participating members often from many companies, suppliers, manufacturers, distributors, and retailers. Membership in the virtual project team has emerged to be so important that companies are often not as effective if they do not participate in virtual project teaming.

Virtual project management teams take advantage of an electronic infrastructure, enabling teams to work in parallel, having continuous access to information, participating from wherever it makes sense, bringing new team members up to speed via the online record of documents, and allowing for team learning. Virtual teaming also involves tapping into world-class competencies that can be accessed electronically. This can be seen in news networks as they assemble ad hoc teams of experts to provide real-time commentary and analysis of the latest breaking news stories around the world. The perspective of teaming includes specific beliefs, knowledge, skills, and behaviors that must converge into a cohesive team to work successfully to overcome time, distance, and cultural constraints.

Support Characteristics for Virtual Environments

The physical infrastructure, the wiring, the local area network (LAN), and the wide area network (WAN) comprise the virtual office, lab, meeting place, and shop floor, and the infrastructure must allow for non-real-time as well as for real-time communications for virtual teams to be successful. The infrastructure must be reviewed on an ongoing basis to ensure that it provides the necessary transport for the team's evolving requirements.

The corporation must pride itself on being highly technology based, thereby supporting new innovations to better improve communications. The virtual corporation must be LAN connected and WAN accessible, and this connectivity must provide virtual project team members with the ability to communicate with one another whenever and wherever necessary. It also means that files and information must be stored in such a way as to make retrieval from remote sites easy and less cumbersome. A virtual corporation views the sharing of information as critical to its success. Therefore, it places a high priority on the flexibility of information access and requires its networks to be developed and maintained with this requirement in mind.

Virtual corporations themselves must be innovative in order to become industry leaders able to maintain their edge. Executives must understand the value of the virtual project team and its members and the autonomy necessary for these teams to be successful. The virtual corporation relinquishes direct control of its project teams, infrastructure designers, and builders in order to achieve the results it seeks. At the same time, it continues to reevaluate core competencies and uses outsourcing when appropriate, and these outsourced resources often become a temporary part of the virtual corporation and virtual project teams.

Comparing Processes and Communications for Traditional and Dispersed Teams

Virtual processes are typically designed for simultaneous electronic information access, rather than serial information flow, to enable team members to see the work developing through the sharing of online information. They can view information and reach an understanding regarding all work in progress, allowing them to anticipate problems and negotiate solutions while the work is still being completed, thereby eliminating the costly rework-after-completion syndrome. An example of this might be a project that utilizes outsourced resources, such as consultants, contractors, or industry specialists, as virtual team members. These members could use electronic information transfer and network infrastructure to track and evaluate the technical specifications while designing the delivery methodologies. The two efforts could evolve in parallel, even though they would occur at different locations, and be dependent on one another.

As with traditional project management teams, the assessment of virtual team processes and work outcomes vary among teams. Once team consensus on communications and reporting is reached and the level of satisfaction attained, the degree of task integration becomes achievable. Task approaches, milestones, and document structure and preparation are all topics that must be discussed by the virtual team. Once common documentation is decided, the teams seem to collaborate better, revealing that standards are necessary in order to set expectations and communications strategies. It has been shown that without these common agreements, conflict and confusion are more likely, and a greater emphasis is placed on physical interaction.

Electronic socialization becomes a factor when collaboration in written form is involved. Delivery of collaborative documents shows that teams can socialize enough to produce something together and thus exhibit a level of cohesiveness. Also, if the expectation is that all members have E-mail for communications, then determining how often mailboxes should be checked is crucial. It is important to promote a positive virtual project team attitude by communicating in a friendly, humorous, and enthusiastic way about the project. E-mail protocols are needed for team cohesiveness. Sometimes sending funny images via E-mail is an important communications message. Addressing one another by name, adding personal remarks, responding to E-mails, and administering support for each other's comments and deadlines are important. Although communication is not the only factor in collaboration, team members must communicate well in order to collaborate well. In a virtual team, common language and technologies are often required for a successful effort. Team members are usually stimulated by speaking with their teammates from different cultures, learning from one another, and feeling the excitement of communicating and sharing knowledge with others around the globe.

Information technology plays a critical role in reshaping the networked organization, yet electronic networks will not replace face-to-face relationships, and this is most evident in virtual project teams. There is definitely a tolerable ratio between face-to-face communications and electronic media exchanges. Effective technology-based collaboration requires the ability to comfortably socialize using technology. Visual cues, in any form—facial expressions, pictures, and so on—videotapes, or videoconferencing assist virtual teams to better communicate with one another. A project kickoff should be face to face; project status, collaborative work, and sharing of information can be electronic. Scheduled face-to-face meetings, videoconferencing or real time, should be interspersed quarterly to ensure trust, familiarity, and teamwork.

Although they share some similarities in this area, a virtual corporation and a traditional one are also very different. The virtual corporation doesn't need dedicated space in order to be functional, although some may be designated for back-office operations. Employees work from home, on the road, in hotels, in airline clubs, or wherever it makes sense to work. The way that they communicate is critical; with a distributed staff, communications are vital to success. A virtual corporation depends on its technologies—voice mail, E-mail, fax, Internet, or intranet—for sharing information and communicating. The employees *are* the company, thus wherever each resides is a company location. As with traditional project management team members, keeping them connected, informed, and highly motivated is the key to a virtual corporation. But the task is more difficult, yet also more rewarding, in a virtual environment.

The virtual corporation often has offices worldwide or utilizes the assistance of others as partners in projects, solutions, processes, or in whatever form the end result takes. The virtual corporation conducts its business in this way, as well as its projects that have specific time and budget constraints. It is possible and even advisable to build virtual alliances with participants from multiple organizations. A consortium of suppliers on a common manufacturing project can connect companies in a way not possible in a traditional environment. Even within the boundaries of a single large corporation, virtual teams can form and reform using a collaborative framework.

Virtual Communities

E-mail usage already exhibits a collaborative behavior in large campus or multi-site corporations. Although 61 percent of all E-mail traffic is destined to stay within the same site or campus location of most typical corporations, 30 percent travels outside the site or campus location, and 9 percent travels outside the corporation itself. The estimate is that by the year 2000, nearly 50 percent of all network priorities will be externally focused. Even more dramatic will be the ability for individual users to construct virtual communities in an ad hoc fashion. Some products are already pioneering this type of workgroup participation model using existing E-mail links between participants. Different from the current usage of groupware titles, these new decentralized titles will support the formation of virtual teams without assistance from technology experts. Increased ubiquity for groupware deployments is on the horizon.

The explosive growth of the World Wide Web (WWW) provides an example of how user-procurable software can accelerate virtual communities and operations. There are over 6,000 new Web sites per month installed outside corporate firewalls, and there is increased demand within corporations for Internet applications that allow information access from the Web. This is an example of *build it and they will use it*.

There are many companies who have realized that they are virtual, that they have distributed teams and staff and function quite effectively in this manner. MetLife is one company that made the transition from traditional in nature to virtual in operations. MetLife's chairman launched a major campaign to transform the corporation into a virtual one. He realized that in order to stay competitive and effective this dramatic change was necessary.

MetLife focused on the company's core business of *helping people become more financially secure* and formed Metra-Health, a giant healthcare company, in partnership with Travelers. MetLife also formed a new business, MetLife Express, to improve the performance—cost, revenue, and investment return—of the core business. MetLife set up an integrated, temporary, virtual team across traditional organizational boundaries to identify the best ideas for the changes. It was a team that would ensure that the effect of implementing the new culture on the enterprise was successful. This high-level virtual team set five sub-teams to pursue opportunities and assist in implementing the virtual corporation concept. These teams focused on retail, customer service, investment return, information technology, and staff services. The first phase took six months to implement, during which time the virtual teams met, shared opportunities and issues, and prepared for weekly management review of progress. The chairman was kept abreast of the progress during this transition period.

The participants of the high-level virtual team were executives with high credibility and communication skills; this is critical if any organizational change is to be successful. The changing organization identified new and responsible owners for improvements and major areas for virtual teaming opportunities. The sub-teams became so effective that the project dimension seemed to fade as they became more of an integral part of meetings with line and staff organizations.

While the change initiators have not been without challenges, the current indications are that they have been successful with the company's transition. They have been able to position themselves for growth, industry consolidation, and internal expansion. By holding firm to core competencies and outsourcing, selling, or partnering with other company competencies, MetLife was able to streamline operations and become a more virtual corporation. *This change would not have been as successful if it had not been initiated and supported by top levels of management in the corporation.* The vision for a more virtual organization was implemented throughout the enterprise because management was clearly behind the initiative.

Characteristics of Virtual Teaming

Productivity is one of the main advantages on which companies focus when considering becoming virtual. A recent *Business Week* cover story documented a General Electric plant in Salisbury, North Carolina, United States, which used virtual work teams and process innovations to achieve a 250 percent increase in productivity! This degree of improvement is quite exceptional, of course; most companies moving to the virtual team concept report 20 to 40 percent gains in productivity after eighteen months. The implementation methods and the dedication of resources for this effort often determine the degree of change. The degree of freedom and flexibility used by the virtual team leadership is also a significant factor. Flexibility is the ability to change when necessary, to make decisions and correct those that may have been wrong, see opportunities and act on them, and encourage others to take chances.

Economists have been saying for years that in order to succeed in a world market, companies must be capable of producing small batches of tailored products on a tight schedule to meet growing demands in emerging markets. This practice calls for innovative technical procedures and team members who move easily from project to project. Virtual team members who have experienced and enjoyed virtual project teams have the skills, information, and motivation to adapt to change. This type of teamwork can enable a corporation to respond quickly to changing conditions both in the organization and in the market.

Quality is only as good as the corporation's commitment to continuous improvement. Virtual project teams help drive quality improvements and new work methodologies into every part of the corporation. When they assume more operational responsibility they develop the ability to see areas of improvement more quickly, clearly, and easily. Virtual project team members bring a fresh look at organizations, processes, and team activities. It is often as if an outside consultant was hired to independently observe operations and make recommended improvements. Analyzing work processes in search of improvement is not only a way of life for virtual teams, it is an ongoing mission, and it is contagious.

Commitment by employees to the company, to a project, to goals, and to objectives is always a challenge for corporate management. Company after company implementing virtual project teams reported finding that increased team involvement breeds increased commitment to corporate-wide goals.

Dedication tends to remain high as well, partly because companies reward skills and contributions to successful teams. Working in a virtual team brings great satisfaction from developing the best work practices as well as the best products; the commitment to the team is significant, and therefore the dedication to a quality deliverable is, as well. Some day soon the virtual team will be seen as an elite sector within the traditional work force, as a positive place that employees strive to join.

Organizations considering these virtual work teams need a dedicated and courageous champion, usually an executive sponsor, who protects the endeavor and ensures the availability of resources necessary to be successful. This person must be committed enough to withstand the stormy early stages of transition, as well as visible and strong enough to earn the respect and support of groups that might choose to sabotage the virtual team philosophy. Why would people chose to derail an initiative? Possible answers include: if it is misunderstood, not communicated well, the merits and rewards are unclear, or the effort is viewed as a threat to traditional operations.

An Example—Automated Systems Integrator

A few years back an innovative idea was generated for an automated systems integrator. In 1991 a major computer products and services company set out to develop a proposal to become the *automated systems integrator* for an aerospace organization. The organization was forming a joint venture team to design and manufacture a new commercial aircraft, and the systems integrator would be a risk-sharing partner in the venture, not just an outsourced competency. This meant that the outsourced company was an alliance partner in the effort instead of a traditional subcontractor. The initial proposed team consisted of about forty stakeholders—a term that can also be attributed to virtual team members—from different groups within the *proposed company*. By the time the project became a reality, over 200 people representing four companies located in over a dozen states in the United States and six countries were involved directly or indirectly. Team membership was always in flux because of the excitement, challenges, changing competency needs, and people moving to new positions.

The overreaching goal of the team was to deliver a win-win proposal by the deadline date. The aerospace and integration companies would be in a partnering—not supplier vendor or outsourcing—relationship. This meant investment risks in people, equipment, and delayed payments were being shared; therefore, writing a losing proposal by the allied team was inherently unacceptable. If the proposal was not accepted, all contributors lost. This set the policy that the customer actually would be part of the virtual, alliance-based proposal team.

To become a successful bidder, the challenge was to create a closely knit team representing all required organizational, technical, and administrative competencies. It also meant keeping executive management in all companies informed of progress, involved in avoiding turf wars, and providing support for meeting an aggressive schedule.

Every project team has a strategy for project completion, whether formal or informal, communicated or not communicated. The proposed team consisted of a project manager, who had overall responsibility for the project; the process and technology manager, representing the engineering and work process perspective; and a business and relationships manager, who took a business perspective on the proposal and facilitated the relationship between the team and the customer. The kickoff meeting, facilitated by the project manager, was held in a facility near the customer site. About forty people from the partnering organizations attended the meeting and determined that in order to provide the right resources, demonstrated competencies were important. Team members agreed to the goals of the project and decided that teams would be created in ten key skill areas, which, in turn, would comprise an important section of the proposal. Program management led the interactions between the project team and the customer, as well as between the project team and executive management. The technology team developed the technical aspects of the proposal, and the organizational capability team addressed virtual work processes, teaming, communications, and the learning elements of the proposal. These were multi-organizational teams. Besides the customer and the proposing company, there were other alliance partner companies involved at various times proposing applications for inclusion in the technical sections of the proposal.

Communication was obviously the greatest challenge to having the dispersed, virtual teams work well together. Communications specialists presented the idea of using electronic means for communications to support the teamwork. They were empowered to develop a communication infrastructure that would address the team's needs. With designed communications, infrastructure, and protocols in place, team members were able to do a great deal of work at a home base, on the road, at a customer site, or wherever they might be. Since pulling the proposal together involved each team member knowing what the others were doing, a *cascading task model* was used in conjunction with a work breakdown structure (WBS) for reporting. Each team kept track of the activities of one other participating team, reporting relevant activities back to its own team members. This idea meant that the right people would have the right information at the right time; this also meant that information was accessible when it was needed.

Virtual project windows were incorporated into the workflow—that is, high-level reporting from the WBS—to allow executives to view and assess all activities. In addition, a team member was linked to an executive in order to serve as a liaison for information and project clarification, as needed. Team members were also identified to cultivate *friendliness* and neutralize *hostilities* in the executive ranks to ensure executives that the risks of the project were assessed and that all measures were being addressed for success.

The best competencies were often not found within the organizations chartered to provide expertise in certain areas; often the organizations needed to look outside and contract for this expertise. Leaders favored demonstrated skills, as opposed to theoretical knowledge, and if not found within their own organizations, they were found on the outside. As with all virtual projects, all team members needed to be skilled in working electronically both internally and externally and in communicating with distributed team members.

The team accepted the challenge of designing its virtual operations, parallel work processes, teaming culture and protocols, continuous communications, and integrated learning systems. Work tasks were intended to be carried out in parallel, such as gathering input from the customer; testing; finding state-of-the-art solutions for emerging needs; writing skill area proposal sections; administering management; and quality focussing on constantly improving the team's operations. With these sub-processes occurring simultaneously, the team was able to keep the schedule on track.

The result was that this project stands as a successful demonstration of virtual corporations teaming together in a virtual project effort. Many of the participants considered the project to be a leading-edge experience, a personal work triumph, and a unique learning experience. The project was considered such a success that all of the companies involved adopted virtual teaming as part of their corporate cultures.

Multi-Tiered Projects and Virtual Teamwork

Over the last decade, a move toward closer collaborative relationships at all levels of the supply chain—the supplier-customer relationship—has been apparent. Although the need for such relationships is universally acknowledged, it has not been possible to realize the full potential benefits for many reasons. Some constraints have been technological and cultural when key decisions often are still made conventionally. There seemed to be no apparent way that was cost effective and efficient to share information and communications to support the ever-changing needs of the supply chain. It has become important to identify and differentiate user and organizational needs for distributed virtual teams. Two of the most important factors in this differentiation are the integration of *best of class* software support tools, as well as personal communication and telecommunication tools, and understanding supplier, customer, and organizational needs for improved business processes and their impact on time to market.

Open participation and communication are critical to a virtual team's success. When participation is accomplished through management selection, mandated incentives, or coercion, the virtual team's success may be in jeopardy. People should not be forced to participate in a virtual team. It is definitely more challenging to manage a virtual product or service development team effectively, especially when team members are geographically dispersed. Forcing people to participate in a virtual team does not add simplicity to this management challenge. The responsibility and requirement of keeping team members up to date on status and creating a sense of real-time unity and trust are critical.

Corporate Examples

AMS Corporation is dedicated to allowing its work force to conduct work wherever is best for the individual. AMS, a company that provides customized software systems to private and public institutions, manages dispersed teams. The company's system development and consulting work requires intense interaction and collaboration with customers located around the world. While some AMS members must be physically located at the client site, it is impractical for the entire team to be there. Thus, AMS is continually finding ways to improve communication and effectiveness for virtual project teams with dispersed geography. A variety of communication technologies is utilized that facilitate group work and play an integral role in supporting teams. As AMS is quite dedicated to supporting its worldwide customer base, it is equally dedicated to supporting its virtual project teams.

European Automotive Manufacturing seems like a unique place to find virtual teaming. A trial is being conducted to set a framework for virtual integration—or a *collaborative working* environment—for the entire European automotive supply chain, including manufacturers; first-, second-, and third-tier suppliers; and automotive companies. A unique and innovative concept, this trial will utilize a variety of leading-edge multimedia interactive systems, product libraries, and distributed decision support. It will be tested through three regional centers in the United Kingdom, Italy, and Ireland.

The key issues are inclusion of the multi-tier suppliers and integration of complex applications, such as CAD, across heterogeneous and public networks into the project. High tariffs exist between the countries for broadband communications, confidentiality, and security issues, as well. Deregulation of country-owned telecommunications has not yet occurred worldwide. The user-driven requirements need to be addressed, demonstrated, and validated, utilizing leading-edge technologies. There ultimately would be a showcase for this trial, and it would set an example for other multi-tiered manufacturing industries for future development efforts. New business processes that would lead to improved time to market and quality of information and products need to be developed. Reviewing each company's existing processes and evaluating them against the team's needs were major requirements. The team objectives were many, as highlighted in the following section.

Team Objectives. To introduce the various key players in the automotive supply chain to the concepts and benefits of cost-effective, leading-edge computing and communications, technologies were needed. These key players included the first- and second-tier suppliers and specialty service providers. Assessing the requirements for regional centers and establishing clearinghouses to support the suppliers for whom the cost of new technology was not feasible due to tariffs, hardware, and software costs were challenging endeavors. Developing the organizational, procedural, and security structures essential to support the introduction of virtual project teams within the supply chain was necessary, as well. Also required was repeatedly evaluating the emerging processes via evaluation, user-based test trials, and demonstrations to user companies and other members of the industry. Disseminating and exploiting the results of the project throughout the European manufacturing industry with special focus on second- and third-tier suppliers was needed, and core activities with related deliverables needed to be identified. They included refinement of user and organizational requirements, including the development of potential scenarios; specification development of technical solutions, including platforms, tools, and communications strategies; integration testing and documentation of the technical solutions; and iterative user and technical evaluations with specific emphasis on the validation of requirements in support of business processes at all tiers of the supply.

A major finding—so far—from this trial is that price is the single most important issue to potential automobile industry customers. A user forum was set up to continue achieving a subset of objectives; the objectives are to:

• educate the customer in the principles and practices of charging for advanced services delivered

• enable the customer in development techniques to control costs when the user has real-time control of bandwidth

• influence the selection by the licensed operators of a charging mechanism, which will be seen as fair, accurate, and reliable by the entire user community

• establish the technical requirements of users upon charging schemes and contract mechanisms

• develop adequate pricing models to be used for trials

• develop a provisioning for the user and to test traffic patterns with users

• evaluate user responses and suggestions to the pricing and provisioning processes.

This trial between automotive suppliers and manufacturers is still being tested, and the results have not been tabulated. The expectation is that although there are many hurdles to overcome—tariffs, competition, security, trust, collaboration, country loyalty, and profit—the end result will be positive. It is possible that a subset of this major activity will be completed, evaluated, and modified for reuse in future projects. As in any significant project activity, breaking it into smaller, manageable work packages allows for demonstrated progress. Once suppliers and manufacturers experience interim successes, they will be more open to committing to the entire opportunity in the future.

2

Trends and Drivers

Business Drivers

Business drivers and current trends shape how corporations conduct, manage, and change their businesses. Current trends in the marketplace, the region, and the world can become unique drivers of business for all types of industries. One significant business driver is competition for market share, an important factor for corporations to consider when determining whether to change their traditional operations and become more virtual in nature. It may make more sense to outsource certain areas of the company, areas that are not core competencies, to become a more virtual—a more *lean and mean*—corporation in order to stay ahead of the competition. The current trend is to focus on these core competencies and outsource the areas that do not promote them. In this manner, corporations maintain leadership in their industries by focusing on the very things that make them leaders. Interim workers, contracted personnel, and outsourced employees are examples of virtual operations staffing. In other words, the company reaps the most benefit by selecting some of its work force to be more *on demand* in nature, virtually, for those areas that are better served by outside, non-corporation sources.

Other trends and drivers that are on the rise for a more dispersed work force are contract or non-contract highly skilled knowledge workers. These workers often live miles, regions, states, or even countries away from one another, yet they are part of the same team. They may do their work at their home offices, on the road, at other corporate sites, or anywhere that is convenient. These workers, as virtual team participants, are vital to the project, the operation, and the ultimate success of the corporation competing in the next decade and century.

Companies are finding that using virtual work teams are not only more the norm but actually are more cost effective and definitely more productive. Virtual teams utilize communications technologies in order to accomplish the expected end result without the many interruptions posed by traditional business travel. Traditional travel adds the burden of often wasted travel time, jet lag, and fatigue that is not present in virtual teaming. *Virtual* generally means that it is temporary, i.e., not permanently in place or there only when necessary. As with many traditional project management teams, a virtual team is assembled for a specific project, has a specific and defined scope, and is disbanded once the project is completed.

Differing from traditional teams who reuse the same resources on all projects, these same virtual resources may be on another virtual team; but then again they may not be. Virtual teams can be found in projects involving product development, middle management, executive management, problem solving, implementation, and support. Virtual project teams can be multi-organizational with representatives from research and development, engineering, procurement, customer service, and operations or support. Regardless of primary reporting, the same elements are true no matter where virtual teaming is found: virtual teaming is temporary, has a specific duration and goal, and teams are disbanded when the project or session is concluded.

Sears Roebuck

Sears Roebuck is a good example of a large corporation realizing almost too late the value of core competencies and virtual staffing. Not too long ago Sears expanded and became involved in selling more than its hardware and electrical building supplies, appliances, and home improvement items. It began selling car, home, and life insurance and reselling usage on its network. The company neither knew what its core competencies were, nor did it know whom its actual customers were. None of these business lines was successful because Sears customers either did not expect the company to be capable in these lines, or they already had sources to satisfy these needs and expected Sears to stick with providing core products.

The competition that Sears faced in insurance was quite fierce, as it was competing against long-established insurance companies with triple-A ratings. As a result of offering intangible products instead of its usual tangible ones, this line of business never delivered to expectation. Thus, Sears has subsequently given up on selling insurance. The company also failed miserably in trying to sell network time and competing against AT&T, MCI, Sprint, and other data network providers. Although the Sears network is still in place and supporting its own business locations, the company no longer has a sales force for, nor views, the network as a product. Sears refocused its efforts on selling its core competencies, which are consumer-tangible commodities instead of intangibles. The company also did a marketing study and realized that its primary customers were women; therefore, Sears added more women-focused products to its retail mix.

Virtual Talent and Resources

Corporations that view themselves as being virtual in nature often utilize resources from outside their own corporations to provide talent in areas where they may be weak, such as virtual project members for temporary management of projects or to outsourced providers for Internet access and related work. They have developed Web sites and outsourced provider access into areas that are necessary for shared communication. There is, via the Web, intranet access to company-related information for the virtual team or outsourced resource utilizing a secured access methodology. These access methods provide for the sharing of vital information among those who are physically dispersed yet need access.

Access to information is absolutely critical for virtual corporations, particularly for those companies wishing to keep their competitive edge. In many instances the talent required to complete a project or become a team resource is not available locally. Company executives in the Midwest United States often mention the scarcity of local talent for technical work. By utilizing virtual employees with the needed skills, the proximity of the talent becomes less important.

Evaluating the virtual team member's contribution and deliverables becomes the underlying factor instead of the number of times a conversation takes place at the coffee machine, or how often the resource has been seen in a day. In today's fast-paced, global world the need for resources to participate in high-impact, time-sensitive projects is growing rapidly. Companies that use technology to link staff are finding themselves 8 to 15 percent more productive than they were before. Acquiring the local skilled workers is often not the best choice; choosing the right workers for a virtual team is. Sometimes cross-functional resources—that is, resources from different parts of the same company or from separate companies—are the best choice for the project. Gathering resources from different organizational functions and totally different organizations brings the knowledge and experience to bear, although it often creates many new challenges for the project manager and project sponsor. The benefits, however, far outweigh these challenges.

What type of resources work best in a virtual project team is an important consideration for project managers. Resources that communicate effectively without the face-to-face contact are critical. This means that team members must communicate their points of view and personalities through electronic resources such as audio conferencing, videoconferencing, the Internet, and E-mail. They also need to have strong verbal and written skills and be willing to act as initiators for communication. In addition, they need to be good problem solvers able to generate solutions remotely and independently.

The Space Program

The United States (U.S.) space program has long been a supporter of distributed project teams. Let us examine one typical project that utilizes this concept. Initially, understanding the various elements of work and identifying the staffing must be accomplished, so the project must first be broken into elements of actual work, and a work breakdown structure (WBS) must be developed. Separating the specific work areas or sub-projects enhances identification of specific skills needed for each work product. The best way to illustrate this is to identify work areas or sub-projects of the WBS. There will undoubtedly be an instrument project, an environmental project, a chassis project, and an engine project, each of which comprises elements of work that focus on the scope of each sub-project. The experience and skill sets that are required for each of these sub-projects would be different; therefore, co-locating all these projects and team members makes little sense and could be quite costly. It is quite possible for the instrument panel engineering to occur in Indiana (U.S.) or in Istanbul; the team can and should use the best skilled resources, wherever they may be located. The same logic holds true for all of the other sub-projects and team members. The challenge is keeping the dispersed project teams in communication so that they know when their elements of work, or tasks, are due and necessary, as well as what other groups are doing that might have dependencies related to theirs. The space program has been very successful in bringing resources into projects from other locations, companies, and industries to develop and build space travel components on time and on budget.

The virtual project team is ideal for these types of projects. A project is planned and funded; tasks, deliverables, dependencies, and resources are identified. The types of resource skills necessary usually have been identified, as well. Finding the appropriate resources from within the same organization includes explaining the scope and duration of the project and negotiating with managers for the resource's devoted time to this effort. If resources are neither available nor qualified, then the outside search for skilled resources should commence. In large, complex, traditional development projects the resource may be dedicated to a project for multiple years, thereby eliminating the opportunity of using this resource on any other projects. The same basic concepts hold true for resources from various companies that will comprise the virtual project teams. These resources might be the best in their fields and therefore much sought for project work. Securing them for this project will take time, and often the project may be under way before they are available to begin. Yet, by utilizing a virtual project team, resources are freed from these constraints and are often able to work on more than one project at a time.

Value Streams

Value streams, a term first coined by James Martin in 1995, are another form of virtual teaming. One way to think of corporations is in terms of value streams, which are end-to-end collections of activities that deliver a result. The value streams within a company correspond to its natural business behavior.

Some value streams—such as product design, customer engagement, distributed logistics, manufacturing, and marketing—are primary activities of a corporation. Other value streams are needed for basic support of the business; they enable the business to operate and are virtual members of the delivery process. Internal-support value streams include purchasing, operational finance, human resources, facilities management, and information technology services. Most of the primary value streams have customers external to the enterprise, whereas the support value streams have customers internal to the enterprise. Good use of networked technology, the Internet, and intranet activities have important effects on virtual teams that operate within value streams. Some of these are examined in the next paragraph.

The team can interact directly and constantly with its customers, including those that are far away. It can respond instantly to customer requests in real time by utilizing technologies, such as electronic data interchange (EDI) and messaging for communications. The team is more self-sufficient because it can access information, expertise, and special-interest communities whenever and wherever it needs this information. It usually does not have to pass work to other departments in the corporation. The team can use powerful tools and interact with distant people using the same tools internally and externally. Given available access to knowledge and computer power, the team can be small and fast moving.

The design of high-performance teams is a particularly important aspect of value stream reinvention. The Internet and all of its resources can greatly increase the capabilities of the self-sufficient, virtual team. The team can be geographically scattered if necessary and quite often is. The team members can be better informed and more aware of the competitive strategies by having access to the latest information. Expert systems can be designed to improve the effectiveness of these virtual teams. Virtual operations in which the team uses certain external resources as though they were internal can be easily designed. It may use resources in countries with low salary requirements, for example, who provide the right skill set for the job at hand. Multi-corporate teams can connect core competencies from different organizations and provide corporations with the edge over their competition.

Hewlett-Packard

Hewlett-Packard is an example of a company that embraces this concept. Hewlett-Packard reengineered itself to minimize the time between having a product concept to having cash flow from customers. For new printers, for example, the concept-to-cash time was cut from four-and-a-half years to twenty-two months and then driven down to ten months without sacrificing quality. Products were redesigned so that they could be manufactured in a more automated way, cutting as many manual steps as possible, while also lowering the possibility for manufacturing defects. Hewlett-Packard created value stream teams and virtual teams that could integrate cross-functional activities and thereby streamline the operation. It is continually reviewing this approach and making the necessary changes as needed. Hewlett-Packard is satisfied with its approach to virtual teaming.

Competition as a Business Driver

It is quite evident that competition is one of the key business drivers for promoting virtual corporations and virtual teaming. As corporations observe competitors utilizing more creative and more cost effective ways to conduct business, they realize that in order to maintain their positions in the marketplace, they too must embrace some of these changes. The changes often have to do with the gathering and disbanding of teams, whether internal or external; the goal is to find the best resources to do the job or the project.

Corporate Examples

There are many corporate examples of the use of virtual teams or distributed work force with excellent results. LM Ericsson is a very good example of a company that has embraced the virtual teaming philosophy and is a known industry leader. It is a virtual corporation with work teams staffed from around the world. It has 17,000 engineers in forty research centers located in twenty countries. This truly symbolizes a commitment to seek resources from wherever is feasible for the job. There are development teams in Australia that work closely with English teams on the same design, although with different work schedules; they collaborate on the actual design in order to achieve a more global product and a more global perspective. The company does some of its manufacturing in China, where the cost of labor is low, and the availability of skilled workers is high. It prides itself on being a global company that not only uses virtual project teams but utilizes virtual design and manufacturing around the clock. Having team members add their input while other team members sleep is quite an efficient use of the workday. When the second team gets to work, the work accomplished during the night is continued, thereby utilizing a twenty-four-hour workday.

Del Monte Corporation is another company that has adapted the virtual concept into its charter. The company is very involved in electronic commerce and is a virtual, *just-in-time* supply partner with its retail outlets. It uses daily inventory reports from grocery stores for restocking and inventory control. Every transaction that is made at a point of sale machine at every grocery store across the country is transmitted and shared with Del Monte to ensure that its products are always available. This prompts a question: When was the last time you went to a grocery store and did not find the Del Monte item that you wanted? Electronic stocking, based on preset ordering thresholds, is also used by Del Monte to eliminate consumer disappointment and the opportunity lost from not having items on the shelves and available in the marketplace.

British Petroleum also took the time to investigate how being more virtual would make it more competitive. British Petroleum in America took an internal look at electronic commerce and at its own virtual corporation because the company wanted to eliminate duplication and over-purchasing of products and services. It was clear that the company needed to automate how purchases were tracked. British Petroleum set up virtual teams to research, develop plans, and implement systems to track purchasing throughout the company and utilized these virtual teams to assist in changing the way the organization made decisions. British Petroleum decided to utilize the corporate network infrastructure and acquire the additional technology necessary to track orders and the status of 440,000 monthly invoices electronically. It set a baseline prior to implementation to see where duplication was occurring and to be able to compare it to changes after adding technology and functionality. The results were reviewed and compared to the baseline after the virtual teams implemented the new systems. Clear benefits were seen. British Petroleum found that by implementing these changes, duplicate purchases were practically eliminated, thereby saving money and time and improving efficiency.

Wal-Mart Stores sets the tone for true virtual commerce. A retailer that has changed the course of supply and demand and redefined the definition of a virtual corporation, this company wanted to achieve an inventory replacement goal of getting goods on the shelves at the lowest price possible. To achieve this goal, Wal-Mart needed a very complex logistics system, one that would buy goods in bulk in the right quantities at the right time.

The company began by taking information from cash register bar code readers and transmitting it to the central control computer. As a crosscheck, inventory was monitored electronically; this also was done with bar code readers. Wal-Mart built a system called *cross docking*, in which goods coming into a warehouse are selected, replaced, and dispatched to stores. The warehouse became a switching center for goods rather than a storage facility. Cross docking enables Wal-Mart to buy entire truckloads of goods at lower bulk prices and then quickly dispatch these goods to stores, essentially eliminating inventory holding costs. In order to be effective and achieve these results, Wal-Mart's systems needed a continuous flow of information from every point of sale machine to its distribution centers and 4,000 vendors. An elaborate computer network choreographed the rapid movement of goods, not only ensuring that the stores had the goods wanted by customers but that holding costs were also minimized wherever and whenever possible.

For a time, Wal-Mart replenished goods on store shelves faster than the industry average while achieving lower holding costs and bulk discounts at the same time. In addition, the store computers provided store managers with detailed information about their specific customers' buying behaviors, enabling informed decisions regarding stocking and new items to be made. Then Wal-Mart went one step farther. It built computer links to its suppliers to enable them to know real-time inventory on their goods and replenish them as needed. Wal-Mart allocated shelf space to these suppliers and paid them only after customers bought the goods, so it was up to the suppliers to keep the shelves stocked. This ability allowed suppliers to manufacture or stock only the items that sold in each store and thus reduce or eliminate the stock on those items that do not sell as well. This dramatic step for Wal-Mart resulted in tremendous cost savings, as it pays for merchandise only as the stock moves instead of tying up funds for inventory. Having this close a relationship with suppliers, Wal-Mart is able to keep shelves stocked, inventory costs low, and successful products available. In addition, it has identified the areas of its business that could be outsourced to others or partnered with suppliers. To date, Wal-Mart has achieved zero inventory-holding costs through this method, and their suppliers have better store and customer-focused goods for sale. By utilizing electronic data interchange (EDI) links to suppliers, Wal Mart's suppliers are able to see every transaction at the exact time of purchase.

Wal-Mart Stores is now using the Internet for the development of additional market share. It began by launching an Internet storefront for online purchasing and is now planning a massive online presence that would make it one of the largest retail destinations on the Web. By November 1997, it expected to offer more than 80,000 different products for sale online. That's more than can be found in one of its typical 110,000-square-foot retail stores! This offering will bring the business of sales, supplier support, and marketing to a new industry height. Most

Internet commerce today is for more expensive items; the Wal-Mart idea is for most commodities sold via Wal-Mart stores. The opportunity for its virtual partners to increase sales is dramatically improved as well. The more Wal-Mart is enhanced visibly, the more its suppliers sell, making it a true *win-win* relationship. Existing relationships with manufacturers and suppliers and their virtual partners may be used to give Wal-Mart the pricing and logistical edge in its Web retailing. Although the company may handle some of its inventory from its own warehouse, it plans to increase usage of EDI links that would allow passing customer orders directly to its suppliers; these manufacturers can then ship products directly to the customers. It should be noted that this method is yet another cost-saving way for Wal-Mart to reduce inventory and shipping expenses. It would make Wal-Mart more of a clearinghouse instead of a retailer. See for yourself; check out Wal-Mart's Web page at *wal-mart.com* and read about its latest idea for its innovation network.

Barclay's Bank prides itself on being a virtual corporation offering virtual banking worldwide. It has many offices throughout the world and shares customer information globally. Barclay's realized that by allowing customers the ability to bank anytime, anywhere, via virtual banking, it could increase customer service as well as profits. Virtual banking is achieved by using computers, automated teller machines (ATMs), and video kiosks for loans, mutual funds, and international money transfers. Barclay's network was recently upgraded to accommodate worldwide transfers, and the company set up Web access for computer usage as well. Barclay's realized that communications and information access were required in order to be a successful virtual corporation.

Singapore's United Overseas Bank LTD, also a virtual corporation, has included stock purchasing in its virtual equation. Its offices issue stocks from *any* automated teller machine within its network. Its goal is to offer the ability to conduct stock transactions from any ATM machine. This is truly a leading-edge concept that will make competitors stand up and take notice!

Citibank, a bank with offices throughout the world, makes it possible for a banker in any Asian branch to see a specific customer's account regardless of in which branch that account is located. To enable this functionality, Citibank had to review its existing network and associated technologies and set up virtual teams to design and implement systems that would accommodate this idea of virtual banking and more robust customer access. In addition, Citibank's Hong Kong branches offer accounts and money in ten different currencies. Customers are able to make transactions at any one location and between locations because Citibank is a virtual corporation that, although dispersed, has access to all necessary information when needed. Citibank, the first to offer home banking, has a Citibank channel that offers home banking for bill paying, funds transfer, loans, and even stock purchases. It provides customer mobile phone access to inquire about the current exchange rate for checking, for money transfers, and for purchasing bank products from its computers and televisions. Citibank has directed its energy toward the idea of anywhere access in hopes of making this its edge on the competition.

Banc One, based in Columbus, Ohio, United States, set out to reinvent its strategic capabilities. Its president wanted to reverse decades of traditional banking by being *in the information business, not the transaction business.* Instead of viewing the business as transaction based, he began seeing it as information based. He wanted the bank to know everything there was to know about its customers. Interestingly, most banks know remarkably little about their customers—except for a piece of their financial bases—or much about customers in general. Customer records normally exist with incompatible data structures on multiple computer systems, some for transactions, savings, home mortgages, and still others for less mainline bank functions. Different, incompatible systems recorded different types of loans; therefore, it was often difficult to know if a customer is or was wealthy or had borrowed from many other sources. This incomplete customer profile could prove costly if the customer had been a credit risk and was now requesting a sizable loan. Banc One set out to create computer systems to coordinate all relevant information about a customer and thereby provide opportunities to cross sell, help avoid bad loans, and provide better services to customers. Armed with such a system, bankers could spend their time deepening relationships with customers, offering true customer service. The system would also facilitate highly targeted marketing campaigns to add to Banc One's market expansion efforts.

Banc One's goal was for its bankers to form and keep deep connections in their local business communities, backed by the best nationwide information system. Local bank presidents could run their operations in their own ways, setting prices, making credit decisions, and serving their communities with the flexibility of the best small banks. The central organization provided automation support and constantly sought to improve bank practices. Banc One set out to achieve the best mix of local employees and central support, and local bankers spent time learning how to serve their communities better. Meanwhile, central management learned how to automate, reengineer, and constantly improve operational practices.

This dream was not an easy one to implement. The Banc One system was very expensive to build, but the company considered that once it worked well in one bank, it would take over at other banks. It could make Banc One more profitable by putting in place its own hardware, software, and knowledge and by intensively training its officers. Banc One spent money in order to meet the goal of being in the information, rather than the transaction, business and, at the same time, set the standard for customer service in banking. Although this concept took both time and money, Banc One has achieved dramatic results. It has transitioned into an information business although its dreams of dramatic market share increases have not materialized at present.

Ameritech Cellular Services, one of the main cellular service providers in the United States, has experienced tremendous growth, and it has taken a technology leadership role in the wireless segment of the telecommunications industry. An initiative launched by this cellular service provider was to establish a leadership position in the wireless data business. Its goals included generating revenues from products and services and stimulating and capturing new traffic volumes generated by data applications that utilize Ameritech's cellular network. As the project matured, identifying and building relationships with partners and collaborators became a necessity, and bringing the first offering to market required interactions with several companies. Among the first stakeholders were AT&T, Paradyne, Anderson Consulting, NEC, AST, Business Partner Solutions, Evtek, Sphere Systems, Tech Data, and Verifone. Some of these partners were hesitant and had issues with trust, authority to make decisions, and inability to see the long-range advantage of the virtual team. Many hours of negotiating and joint decision-making were vital to the success of this endeavor.

The outcome from this project is interesting. Early, the majority of time and effort was spent on building and maintaining the virtual relationships. Later, the focus was on operating details such as product management, marketing, advertising, and promotional materials. Toward the end of the project only 15 percent of time was spent in sustaining virtual relationships.

There were very real and unanticipated problems with this project, such as ownership of the deliverables. Who owned the product? Who marketed the product? Where were their royalties? Eventually these were ironed out, and the alliance partners were in agreement. These issues notwithstanding, this was a successful product launch with a virtual team of partnered corporations, but the essential ownership issues were not resolved until the end of the project, which, in retrospect, should have been anticipated.

Digital Equipment Corporation has employed virtual project teams whose members were located throughout the United States to develop computers by sharing databases, simulations, and modeling for a long time. This concept meant that the design was occurring in many places simultaneously and that a high-speed network with significant capability was necessary for the transport and communications. In addition, computer-to-computer videoconferencing was important in order for the dispersed teams to share the drawings and communicate real time. Digital became so good at managing these virtual design teams that it even conducted seminars for customers with members from its marketing group to teach these skills. Digital has paved the way for collaborative development. (Note: At this writing, Digital is being acquired.)

BESTNET, a consortium in California (United States) and Mexico, collaboratively teaches Spanish and English. This company had its trainers attend classes to ensure that they would all be trained and would teach the materials in the same way. BESTNET utilized videoconferencing to produce virtual training classes, as well as to share teaching experiences. It felt this to be a vital element in its teaching philosophy. The classrooms were equipped with videoconferencing technology and capability to allow the inter-country process learning to occur. It also allowed instructors to fill in for others in the event of illness. The session could have a distance instructor, which worked very effectively for its virtual environment.

AT&T, one of the largest telecommunications suppliers in the world, has virtual operations around the world, as well, including designers, technicians, and consultants. Computer-to-computer communication and videoconferencing are used to assist in its global customer support. AT&T depends heavily on this technology allowing sharing of customer information and providing the highest quality inter-country support possible. It uses these technologies for all of its products and services, including its distributed project teams installing high-speed transport worldwide. AT&T has dramatically reduced dedicated office space by having virtual project teams work from wherever it makes sense to work. It believes that this is one reason that it is still a leader in the industry.

3

Piloting

The Need to Pilot

Hewlett-Packard (HP) has a network infrastructure group—as do many large corporations—that researches, tests, and rolls out new infrastructure technologies and services to its internal HP customers. Hewlett-Packard, like other technology companies, follows a life cycle for services that tracks all phases of a service from its inception to its decommissioning. As noted earlier, it, like other large corporations, uses virtual project teams from within its corporate groups, but they report to different managers, divisions, or business units. The philosophy at HP is to utilize the best resource for the job, do the job right the first time, and share best practices whenever possible. There is no need to continue to recreate the wheel.

In rolling out new services, staff knows that it is always important to state the scope, goal, and expectation of the service, test-associated technologies, and the specific service prior to production. The staff understands the reasons for preliminary work; the biggest ones involve meeting user or customer expectations for the service and providing ongoing support after the service has been implemented. If a new service is rolled out without taking these factors into consideration, many things could occur. If the service is inconsistent or not functioning as expected, the division immediately loses credibility regarding its expertise and dependability, the operations support group is bombarded with trouble calls, impacting its support of other services, and the product or service never wins overall support and approval.

The logical question might then be: Why would any group roll out a product or service without adequately testing and perhaps even proto-typing it first? The answer has to do with assuming the risk up front or assuming the risk after the fact, and that answer depends on organizational culture. Hewlett-Packard has strict standards for meeting criteria prior to putting a new service into the production environment. It assesses the risk and decides how great it is, what it will effect, and whether or not it out-weighs the need for the service. How do they do this?

Testing the Culture/Conducting a Pilot

Testing the culture is the first step in knowing if a concept, product, or ser-vice will fit, will be accepted, and can be supported. Corporations need to consider how they will assimilate virtual, distributed project teams into their existing corporate cultures. Some less structured organizational cultures are better ready to do this than others with more traditional structures.

One safe way to test change in a culture is to conduct a pilot. Con-ducting a pilot, simulation, or prototype to see how a virtual, distributed project team functions, and how this change can be integrated into the existing corporate culture, is a good way to test the waters. This chapter covers the steps for conducting a pilot to implement the concept of vir-tual project staffing and management into the environment. To success-fully implement this concept, it will be addressed as life cycles of a service or development effort are explained.

Basic concepts, such as the life cycle of a service or development effort, hold true when piloting virtual project management as well. It too has its life cycle. Let's begin with the basic understanding of a life cycle, that is, from inception to the end of its useful life. Actual life-cycle phases may consist of six phases, for example: brainstorming or idea generation, research or investigation, planning or design, development or testing, sup-port or delivery, and dismantling or discontinuance.

A Typical Six-Phase Life Cycle

Brainstorming or Idea Generation. This phase is often referred to as the brainstorming phase, when ideas are randomly stated and shared. Excitement is generated as each idea spawns another until new ideas have been exhausted. These ideas are then reviewed, discussed, and prioritized, and those that lack support are eliminated. Usually, one or two of the ideas are strong and the team determines whether to investigate one or both. This phase sets the groundwork for future discovery and investigation to research the viability of the ideas.

Assume that an organization had the idea to implement virtual project management. It completed the first phase of the life cycle and now is involved in the research or investigation. Prior to any rollouts that affect the corporate population, the organization prides itself on conducting proper research and testing prior to a corporate-wide rollout.

Research or Investigation. The primary purpose of this phase is to prepare the chosen idea that addresses requirements based on business plans and/or user and customer requirements. It might be a business plan that incorporates risk, costs for research (resource and capital), estimated schedule for research completion, and expectations prior to planning an actual rollout.

In the case of this company, it would be to identify a project that would be piloted with a virtual project team. The project objectives, scope, resource skill, benefit to the organization, and all elements surrounding it must be defined. Project scope limitations—what it is and what it is not—and known risks must also be identified. In this case, the unknown may be the success or failure of the virtual project team concept. Like all other projects, plans for mitigating risks should be addressed.

There are certain objectives for the research and investigation phase. Develop a clear definition of the user and customer needs for the project. Why complete the project in the first place? As in other projects, it is necessary to define requirements in terms of cost, time-to-market, support, and billing. For projects to be successful, team members need to ensure that the project meets 100 percent of the primary needs of the business, users, and customers. All requirements must be addressed from a user/customer perspective. Will it meet the expectations of the user? This is the time to identify and resolve compatibility, interface, and dependency issues. Can the project leverage with existing architectures, hardware, systems, processes, components, resources, and cultural issues?

This phase has certain deliverables that are required in order to proceed further. There should be high-level implementation plans with resource and schedule projections. In some cases, a preliminary functionality specification needs to be developed. What will the project achieve or deliver? How will the specification identify alternatives and goals? Service requirements from the user perspective, including definitions that are complete to ensure that the team resources have a clear understanding of responsibilities, should not be developed at this time.

Planning or Design. Once the research and investigation for the project have been completed and the necessary management approval given, the next phase, planning or design, begins. This is really the time for thinking through how this project and virtual project management will fit and change the existing culture. The purpose of this phase is often to specify products, vendors, components, processes, resources, and infrastructure necessary to deliver a complete product or service. In this case, it would be to address these but also to identify what changes need to be made in the culture, processes, communications, and reporting areas in order for virtual project management to be effective. This information often propagates the project plan necessary to manage the implementation.

One of the key elements here is securing resources for the pilot that are open to change, can work and communicate at a distance, and have the project skills necessary for the actual project work. As this pilot's purpose is not only to deliver a product or service but also to test a virtual team project, staffing is critical. Finding resources from other divisions, states, countries, or companies might be difficult but is often the best way to ensure that qualified resources are chosen. The location of team resources should not be significant; their skills for completing the project should be the priority. Communication among team members involved in the pilot is of ultimate importance and will determine how well distributed teams work within the corporation. Often, once the team has been identified, a communications strategy session must be conducted to ensure agreement in type, frequency, and commitment to team communications.

The design or planning phase has objectives that should be addressed prior to proceeding further. As in all projects, a detailed product or service design needs to be developed. Test plans and testing strategies should be defined and agreed upon by the team. Support plans for delivering the product or service once it has been implemented are critical to address at this stage.

Certain deliverables are also required at this point. Documents that describe the processes necessary for delivering the product or service need to be developed. In this case, virtual project team documents should be developed as well so that the team's process could be reused on subsequent projects. Incorporate initial service functionality into the specification and future capability into the plan. In this project it would be beneficial to identify customer needs and other constraints that could cause problems in the future. This is the time to identify the processes that needs to be developed and begin this effort. One of the preliminary requirements is to identify a support plan. This is necessary for a product or service but equally as necessary when a project team is a distributed one. For example, who sets the distribution lists for the team; develops the meeting agendas, takes the meeting minutes and distributes them to the team; keeps the schedule; and develops the reports? This administrative work often falls upon the project manager. The virtual team members need to understand that their parts of this responsibility are critical to the team's success.

Identify a financial model. How much will it cost for team member participation, new infrastructure for the team, and communications and collaboration tools? What necessary implementation tools need to be developed or purchased? This can be for the actual project, as well as for implementing the virtual project team concept. When all these issues and deliverables have been addressed, and management has approved this phase, the project then proceeds into the development or testing phase.

Development or Testing. This phase follows the development of all planning and preliminary documentation. It will add to the existing documentation to bring it to a point when it could be used in a production environment. The purpose of this phase is to test the actual product or service, as well as the processes and support, against the user/customer requirements. In this case, it is also to test how the virtual project team members are doing in their distributed locations, while delivering a real project to its completion. During this phase most of the ancillary work required to produce a complete product or service is also accomplished. This could include user/customer documentation; user and support staff training; internal documentation for support, as well as processes for duplication; test plan creation, execution, and results; the structure of the production environment, if any changes need to be made to support this product or service; and testing of all components for functionality, usability, reliability, performance, and support.

This phase often consists of more then one pilot: the first pilot may be used to test concepts or vendors to ensure that the expectations, assumptions, and outcome are met. This pilot often has basic, perhaps even manual, processes and limited range for actual testing; perhaps only the project team will participate. The second pilot often is the pre-production pilot or testing that really determines if the product or service meets user/customer and business expectations, as well as support requirements. This pilot is also used to test the scalability of the processes prior to going into an unforgiving production environment.

The first pilot may be the first proof of concept, often called the Alfa, for a new product or service. The scope of this pilot includes how long the pilot will run, how many participants it will include, the costs for purchasing equipment and/or network services, and how the decision to proceed will be determined. This pilot will ensure that the service meets usability, accuracy, and completeness objectives in a user and support environment. This is the time to develop manual processes, address functionality, develop prototype tools, develop draft forms of documentation, and test all of the concepts, designs, vendors, strategies, and requirements in a controlled environment with a limited number of users. This pilot would not be necessary for the virtual project team pilot; an actual project or service should be put through this preliminary step.

The second pilot addresses all pre-production requirements for a new service or product and, in this case, will prove whether or not the virtual team concept can work in the culture. If the product or service cannot feasibly go through a full pre-production pilot, then there may have been a problem with the teamwork. Let's assume that the teamwork has been successful and all areas have been addressed, thereby allowing the product or service to enter and run in this pilot.

This pre-production pilot will ensure that the service meets production standards for usability and supportability in the corporate environment. This is the time when all provision, billing, and support processes; product or service functionality; provisioning or support tools; documentation; concepts; designs; vendors; strategies; and requirements are fully tested. This pilot must be successful—or elements that were unsuccessful corrected—prior to the actual corporate rollout.

This is a pilot that simulates an actual production environment; therefore, it requires all processes and technologies to be tested with production expectations and goals in mind. The processes, rollout risk, design assumptions, and success criteria are validated. Metrics are collected, and contingency plans are tested. This is the time to stress-test all the designs, relationships, strategies, processes, and support requirements prior to rolling the service into production. It is a point of go, no-go decision-making. If it is a no go, you must return to square one and begin the process again with the same or different project objectives. Once this has been reviewed, and management has approved the results, a rollout or implementation can be conducted. This will also allow for any last minute virtual project team deliverables to be completed and the effort evaluated.

Specific objectives for these pilots are as follows.

- In order to ensure that a product or service meets the design specification a pilot is conducted. During this pilot all elements are tested to meet initial strategies.
- Obstacles or showstoppers should be clearly identified and their resolution addressed. Any changes necessary in order to meet production requirements, whether to the infrastructure, support, or culture, need to be identified.
- Testing for performance, configuration, and delivery varieties needs to be done and the results documented. The product or service should be tested across multiple scenarios and under many conditions. During this testing all interfaces and dependencies need to be identified and evaluated.
- The actual pilot documentation must include the scope and expectations so that the success or failure of the pilot can be evaluated.

Once the project has the fundamentals in place—such as sponsor, team, objectives, and goals of the pilot—the planning, design, and implementation take place. The development and distribution of project plans are important to be able to track the progress of the pilot's scope. During the pilot, a benchmark should be set to compare the progress, pitfalls, constraints, and resolutions; this will also be necessary when evaluating the pilot. This is also the time to identify the technology and infrastructure, resources, support, and processes necessary for a production environment. After conducting the pilot and reviewing the results, it is easier to plan for the rollout to the entire enterprise.

Assessing the Pilot

After conducting the pilot, it is time to assess its success or failure in the operation. The pilot must be evaluated in terms of how well the product or service was implemented, of course, but how the actual virtual team worked as independent contributors should also be examined. One of the most important elements to consider is how selecting team members from other groups, not co-located, positively or negatively impacted the project.

All previous pilots have been conducted and their results studied, changes made, and approval achieved for rolling out this new product, service, or, in this case, concept. As in other projects, complete rollout plans must be developed including the strategy for rollout. Should it be in phases to allow for an area to be completed prior to rolling out to another, or is a company-wide strategy better? In terms of a product or service, often a company-wide approach is necessary because all users and customers will be affected simultaneously. For a virtual project team rollout, it may prove wiser to roll out to high-profile projects or projects in which the logical team members are distributed. In any case, members from the rollout team should include the actual implementers, as well as members from the operations or support organization, to ensure complete coordination and acceptable turnover.

Support or Delivery. Continuous delivery, the support phase, is ensuring that the product or service will be available to users and customers on an ongoing basis. All processes have been tested and are now in the production support environment. As with existing services, the job of ensuring a stable ongoing environment is in place. This is also the place where upgrades and improvements to the service are identified, and their impacts to the production environment are assessed. Often these changes force an investigation and a pilot to assess the impact to the existing environment. This may lead back through the life-cycle steps prior to assessment.

Dismantling or Discontinuance. The final stage is dismantling or discontinuance of a product or service, as needed. Usually prior to this phase another product or service has been introduced and steps have been developed to remove this service from the production environment. In this case, often steps for transitioning users or customers from this product or service to its replacement have been developed, and the actual changes begin to occur. Most users or customers do not object to this change if it is handled in a non-service impacting way, as much as possible. As in other phases, all plans, schedules, and methods need to be reviewed and approved prior to implementing this change.

4

Virtual Operations

What Are Virtual Operations?

Virtual operations are anywhere, anytime tasks, deliverables, processes, and general work. They can be seen in tasks where the value of the work or end product is in itself highly valued, rather than the effort needed to complete the task. It is not how many hours, which hours, and from where the work was achieved, but if the deliverable was on time and if it met team and project expectations that are important.

A good example of this is the autonomy given to college students by their professors. The first day of class they are handed a sheet listing the chapters to be read, when the material pertaining to them is due, the test dates, and the date papers are due. The professor mentions that attendance is unnecessary if students pass the tests and deliver the papers on time. This concept is the same in managing a virtual operation; when deliverables are due is the focus, not where the work is accomplished.

Managing a virtual project team requires more trust than often is given in traditional co-located team management and also needs more support, because the team members usually are not available to communicate daily. This is especially true of multinational project teams in which E-mail across multiple time zones is the only logical communication that works regardless of the hour of the day. Real-time communications and scheduling are more difficult because of the dispersed team's local or native work schedules. This does not mean that these employees or team members have any less need for being part of the corporation. It does mean, however, that they

Table 2. Nine Steps to Virtual Operations

There are nine basic steps necessary for transitioning to virtual operations, as shown by Ray Grenier and George Metes in their 1995 book, *Going Virtual*.

1. **Engaging in the virtual operations idea**: This involves top management initiating a process to examine the current situation, recognizing that its current business could or does exist in a virtual environment.

2. **Creating a vision**: Executive management creates a vision for virtual operations for the organization and formally shares it with the entire corporation.

3. **Weighing all factors and making the decision to go virtual**: Executive management reviews or baselines the current situation and decides that transitioning to virtual operations is the wave of the future.

4. **Building support within the organization**: Management spreads the word and builds consensus among key influencers within the organization, including managers, technical staff, human resources advisors, and contributors.

5. **Including the entire organization**: Management develops a strategy and associated processes to introduce the concept of virtual operations to the entire enterprise. This includes stating the challenges and opportunities, high-level training plans, new processes development, work task evaluation, teaming exercises, communication strategies, and new learning opportunities.

6. **Building a plan and focusing on its success**: Management needs to set the example by offering training, developing publicity, and highlighting on-site leadership; management raises the awareness and buy-in of the value of a virtual organization.

7. **Understanding organizational readiness**: This involves being able to read the indicators of organizational readiness, to gauge the current organizational state, and to guide the transition as a management responsibility.

8. **Creating a formal specification outlining virtual operations**: This involves reviewing the internal environment and selecting two or three difficult areas within the organization that may be suited and ready to work in a virtual environment. It also includes developing a prototype project or pilot that utilizes virtual operations while meeting aggressive business goals for this project.

9. **Choosing a project manager to head up the virtual transition effort**: Select a qualified person to be the project manager to lead a pilot virtual project team in the design of new processes that would meet the specification and deliver the project.

work differently, remotely, and need to be treated, acknowledged, appreciated, and communicated with as frequently as if they were local.

In order for remote team members—or workers in general—to be productive and feel connected, processes and standards must be in place. Processes include those that must be in place for networked communications to be successful. These processes support virtual operations and are designed for simultaneous electronic access. The current ways of communicating must be examined and evaluated as to their value in a virtual enterprise. It might mean that new processes or new ways of communicating information to one another have to be developed in order for the virtual organization to function well.

Virtual Teaming

Teaming is the essence of a project; it is a distinct group of people working together for the same end purpose with tasks and deliverables to complete along the way. The project success or failure depends on a high level of inter-team communications and information sharing. In a virtual project team, with team members distributed globally, technology is an enabler, a special communications tool, for the virtual project team. Audio conferences and E-mail sometimes are the most significant forms of communication that a distributed team can have. Not applying this technology to a global project will surely cause communications, dependencies, and deliverables to falter.

Communications is a designated way of exchanging, accessing, distributing, recording, changing, and sharing information, and a communications strategy must be established at the beginning of the project to set the team's expectations. Communications manners, context, and methodologies are the most critical factors in determining the success or failure of a virtual project team. Supporting technologies, conference bridges, E-mail distribution lists, and remote access to corporate servers must be in place and access allowed, enabling the virtual corporation and the virtual team to function well. The information network infrastructure; LANs and WANs; distributed, accessible information database systems; workgroup communications applications with groupware functionality; file transfer; and database access must be set prior to launching any initiatives for virtual projects. These technologies must be production systems with full support, especially if the corporation and project teams are worldwide and twenty-four hour in nature. The technology infrastructure needs to be

Table 3.   Comparing Traditional and Virtual Processes

Traditional	Virtual
Co-located resources	Distributed, technically connected resources
Serial, sequential work	Parallel, simultaneous at times
Ad hoc communications	Continuous, anytime communications
Face-to-face discussions	Non-real time chat sessions
Paper exchange	Electronic document exchange
Distribution processes	Global access of information
Individual task work	Continuous sharing of tasks and dependencies
Local information storage	Global information repository
Questionable, unworkable processes	Processes that support virtual work
Working solo	Collaboration
Competition and distrust	Teamwork and trust
Decision-making from the top	Team decision-making

monitored and controlled whether it is done internally by the corporation or by an outsourced vendor. The full availability of the technology infrastructure is necessary for distributed teams or staff to successfully communicate and deliver. The establishment of communications standards, directories for voice and data addresses, messaging techniques, security requirements, management, and data storage standards fall naturally under the control and maintenance of these focused organizations. They become a vital part of the virtual operation.

Virtual Learning

Virtual learning is a process during which teams and organizations build knowledge through culture and cross-functional operations. Every project builds on previous experience and learning. This differs from focused or traditional learning when a specific topic is studied for expertise. Often this process of virtual learning is called *unconscious learning* or learning while doing. Why is this important?

Being a member of a virtual project team, or a staff member in a virtual organization, offers tremendous opportunities for virtual learning to occur. Self-sufficiency and autonomy are required in a virtual environment; expecting someone else to supply the solution usually is not an option. This is especially true if distributed staff or project members work remotely in a home office or at a job site. Often *on-the-job* training means that decisions are made and issues are resolved, and the results will be electronically communicated to the team or corporation.

Preparing for the Transition

Transitioning to virtual operations is not an easy step for a traditional organization to undertake. It is far too easy to fall back into traditional ways when virtual processes do not seem to work or when a remote worker is not immediately available. Realizing that communication need not be real time, and that there really is a large window for response, is a change to standard operations.

Knowledge that a real problem exists is the first step in finding a solution to the *old* ways of doing business, or at least an approach to the solution. The real need is learning to transition from the current way of operating and the realization that the transition is a giant step. Understanding the value and workings of an electronic information infrastructure, collaborative relationships with partners and suppliers, complementary competencies, and virtual reengineering all raise the probability that a successful workplace transition will take place. The actual implementation of these virtual capabilities requires action: high-level support and commitment, planning, prototyping, and scaling efforts throughout the organization, as well as the periodic and timely communication of the goals and expectations of a virtual operation to the company.

In order to ensure a successful transition to a virtual corporation and to virtual project teams, value and commitment must be placed on developing and supporting an electronic information infrastructure. The infrastructure is no longer an overhead item to be depreciated and used; it now is a vital information and knowledge transport system critical to the success and often the key to gaining a competitive edge in the marketplace.

Often, collaborative relationships with business partners, suppliers, and companies with complementary competencies is necessary in order to make the transition. Bringing a business partner or supplier into the project as a virtual team member is often the most practical approach for attaining a successful, dependable, knowledgeable, and empowered project team. Some of the most successful projects have included participants from aligned corporations. Success for the corporation, as well as for project teams, requires a high level of support for the day-to-day operations of the team processes. Management must provide commitment for the success elements of early planning to set expectations, prototyping to test ideas, and scaling the deliverables for growth in a production environment.

Continuous management support is imperative to a virtual team's success and to a transition into virtual operations. The transition for software developers often is not about coding or developing software but about the environment in which the developers work, that of being efficient and effective. It is more about people and the inherent virtues of working collaboratively in teams to build a set of common goals, values, and culture than about the product execution when criteria for success is measured. This does not mean that the project is not important; it does mean that if the distributed team is not cohesive, the project's success will be greatly diminished. The cultural aspect of shared values that brings the virtual team together to achieve a common goal to develop a virtual environment is known as *soft technology*. These soft technology cultural aspects are often the primary predictors of the success or failure of a virtual organization. Accepting and supporting cultural changes, values, and common goals are necessary for a successful transition to a virtual organization.

As critical to the success of the cultural change to virtual operations are management support and leadership for the team and the concept of the *best of class* for virtual teaming projects. The individual attitudes of management, leaders, and team members, and commitment to the goal of going virtual and providing all of the resources necessary to get there, will make or break this virtual operations goal.

The knowledge gained by the project team, management, and the organization, if communications took place about the success of the project, would be invaluable. Those who shared this unique experience would gain buy-in for future projects, and support for others would be apparent. There may be the need for multiple pilots; one for every area of the enterprise, as this transition might need opportunities for testing this prior to full acceptance.

There are many considerations that need to be addressed in order for virtual operations to be successful. Management must be willing to look at its existing corporate paradigm and determine if the organization is able to create value in its deliverables or not. It must perform an in-depth analysis of the environment (in weeks instead of months), including defined markets, customer needs, existing projects, and essential relationships. Management needs to better observe its competition and determine if virtual operations will affect the company's position in the industry. If this dramatic change is needed, then management must understand what level of effort is required to successfully make it.

A vision for the new organization paradigm must be created from the executive management layer of the organization and then shared with all levels. Funds must be allocated to support the technology infrastructure buildup, if necessary, to support the transition to more virtual operations. A temporary virtual corporation transition team or task force needs to be identified to ensure that the corporation follows through with the transition and that it is not just another corporate initiative. This team or task force will serve an important role in keeping the organization's attention focused on the objectives while maintaining focus throughout the transition. The task force members also play another role: increasing management confidence and comfort by providing a focal point for identifying and resolving risk. They also could provide the feedback loop into management for changes that should be made whether or not the corporation transitions into virtual operations.

The project leader and the virtual project team members need to be identified early. The leader should have respect from within the organization, believe in the corporate vision, and have excellent leadership skills. The project manager also needs to be willing to make tough decisions, obtain total commitment from both management and individuals, and possess the ability to drive a physically dispersed team. The project manager or leader will proactively monitor the project goals and be part of the decision-making for virtual operations, as well as assist in driving the change through the organization.

The purpose of the virtual project is the responsibility of the key stakeholders, as they define the scope and objectives. Identification and interaction between the project leader, the stakeholders, and special interest group members is key to the success of the project. Agenda content must be agreed upon by the entire project team or by someone with knowledge and experience in the use of complex information and communication processes. The entire team must accept the final design and scope of the project; it must understand its value to the organization. Developing commitment is essential for any project to complete to expectations. One of the best ways to develop commitment required for changing work habits and behavior is to involve everyone in the effort. The project leader is in charge of the project and must ensure that the entire team accepts and approves the final work plan. The goal is that the team will complete a work process plan for transitioning to virtual operations that also will successfully deliver the required results and criteria as specified by management.

Virtual project teams—or any project teams, actually—do not succeed without strong leadership. However, leading virtual teams is far more demanding than leading a face-to-face team; excellent team leadership skills are needed to overcome the challenges that distributed team members create. Like other project team leaders, leaders of virtual projects must be able to motivate the team members by instilling a sense of excitement about the project and the organization, but often at a distance. It is said that leadership is setting an example; this is frequently accomplished through the use of excellent communication skills, the innate ability to work easily with all types of people, the sensitivity to encourage at the right time, and the capability to share the corporate vision effectively. Leaders are often seen as *visionary carriers* who encourage team members to engage in organization development and then step back to become proactive problem solvers. They ask for both strategic and tactical perspectives.

Sometimes there are different leaders for different aspects of the project. An example of this may be seen as projects continue through their life cycles: project coordination leads and technical leads, as well as technology and infrastructure leads. These leads may coexist throughout the project or may exist for brief periods during the project when their leadership and expertise are necessary. They may transition into a resource on the team at a later time.

Current operations must be baselined, providing a snapshot of where the corporation is at present, and a plan for transitioning to virtual operations must be developed. A matrix for comparing old operations and processes to new ones should also be created to track the transition—its successes and its failures. How else could you see if the operation was working better or not? It is also important to obtain buy-in from outside groups that may have to change their working styles and habits as a result of the transition. Successes in this area must be highlighted and shared with the enterprise, as support for others to follow later.

If the operation is open to this transition but requires formal documentation, then a persuasive business case may need to be developed, approved, and shared with the entire enterprise to ensure all groups and divisions know of the impending changes. The argument for virtual operations should provide a basis for executives to continually examine their own convictions. It should include the following:

• The reason for the changes should be related to the corporate vision.
• It should be written in a language that individuals in organizations can easily understand.
• It should outline clearly the effects that the changes will have on the organization.
• As in other business cases, it should be unambiguous in its requirements.
• There should be a clear identification about the benefits, risks, and incentives.

Asking key questions is important; questions such as the following might be considered:

• Has success or failure been clearly identified?
• What are the training tools available, and how will they be provided?
• What are the critical success criteria?
• What are the metrics for evaluating the success criteria of the transition?
• Are the most appropriate delivery mechanisms in place: face-to-face meetings, newsletters, video broadcasts, training, E-mail, and bulletin boards?
• Is the information infrastructure ready for virtual communications? If not, what is being done, and when, to ensure that this is available?
• Is there a non-threatening feedback mechanism in place?

Transitioning to virtual operations means staying on course while taking the traditional corporation in a new direction, one that may appear too unstructured and risky to some. But then again, change itself is considered unstructured and risky by many. Demonstrating early successes is one way of keeping people informed and gaining support for the next steps. As the change moves throughout the organization, the goals must be spotlighted regularly in order to stay on track with the transition.

It is important to adapt and revise existing work practices, such as communications, into the new virtual workplace in order for them to successfully function. Often the normal pace of life will change, as staff moves from being centralized to distributed, as will the decision-making process. The impact of these changes needs to be evaluated and solutions developed. At all levels, virtual work processes contribute to value generation, productivity, and cost reduction in the organization. Early results indicate that reengineering basic business processes for the virtual environment is achieving tremendous results. Rethinking how these are done enables staff to participate and make the processes more usable for them as well. Virtual work environments impose no predetermined limits on the range of the participant's capability. It is the quality of the deliverable that counts.

Virtual Operations

Some examples of what virtual work processes accomplish are as follows. High-quality products and services are being produced, sometimes as high as 50 percent or more, by bringing serial work processes into parallel. Non-dependency driven work occurs whenever there is time. (Note that this idea is not limited to virtual operations or distributed project teams.) Simultaneity in the virtual context is achieved by providing ubiquitous access to information across geographies, disciplines, and cultures. Travel reduction is a direct result of virtual project teams when collaboration has increased by 50 percent or more, and resources are distributed throughout the world. Virtual projects are providing management with real-time information about existing projects, thus providing the opportunity to make immediate adjustments to changes rather than waiting for periodic reporting to trigger interventions. This change process—that of real-time information access—is also a factor in non-distributed project teams. Requiring accessible information that is comprehensive and standard in content is important to the project, and valuable learning tools that can be shared throughout the organization also are important.

It helps to know the difference between traditional ways of doing work and virtual ways. Traditionally, managers have often felt that it is important to have all project participants in the same building, so they can *keep an eye on the scoundrels*. This enabled concentration of tools and materials, facilitated communication, and provided some control for management. Within virtual projects, supported by virtual work processes, a manager may have the ultimate responsibility for projects with teams dispersed worldwide and connected via the network infrastructure. By having the project information available electronically the manager can view real-time project status, ask questions, and carry on conversations through the network, wherever the resources are located. It is quite a mindset change for traditional managers who have to overcome their need for controlling staff and transition into the need to have commitments met.

Historic ways of completing physical development for technology of software, as well as manufacturing processes, have involved sequential or serial fabrication methods and assembly processes, and they often still do. Early information-based work processes like research, administration, and software development and design were based on serial and sequential information flow models. The serial model has major drawbacks in that downstream work—that is, work occurring later in the process—often must wait until the upstream work has been completed and, therefore, has little or no input, knowledge, or often any perspective on the scope or magnitude of the project. There is often no awareness as to the benefits or risks of the project or of places in the project. It follows in this sequential process that errors or omissions in an earlier stage were extremely disruptive in later stages, often causing rework from prior stages that caused delays, or the errors or omissions were passed through to the consumer as a bad or buggy, non-fully functional product. Later versions or patches were released to rectify these bugs, and the consumer was expected to *limp* along or work around these until the fixes were released.

Virtual project management often presents a more holistic view of the workflow environment and can offer alternatives to this serial process. Members begin a project together, viewing the entire project scope in a kickoff-type meeting, so that all members of the team understand the entire project and how their individual pieces fit into this overall puzzle. These teams are often able to break the cycle into more manageable subtasks that can be performed simultaneously once they view the entire project and develop a critical path and dependency model. Many of these subtasks continue in parallel, with information objects being continuously exchanged between the participants to produce a smoother and more meaningful flow of work. This does not preclude that there are always some tasks that must be done in a serial or sequential fashion, but by viewing the entire project, it is easier to load resources into these areas to assist in scheduling and project task flow. In addition, if no supplementary work is added to the effort, meaning that the scope stays constant and additional scope changes are added to a later release, and if the needed resources are available at the designated timeframe, the project work time often could be substantially shortened without sacrificing quality.

Since virtual team tasks are designed around electronic information access, rather than sequential workflow, participants can work, developing and contributing when and where appropriate. They may view the entire work effort, anticipate problems, and negotiate solutions while the work is still upstream, eliminating costly rework. An example is in the sequential model of a document development process. The text is developed by a writer who ships it via E-mail, United States mail, FedEx, or file transfer to an illustrator, who knows that the text provides connection to her illustrations. In a virtual team model, where information access is available, the illustrator has constant access to the text, often as it is being written. It could be in shared databases, Web intranets, or at a computer-to-computer conference, allowing simultaneous viewing of impending text or image problems to be exposed real time. This is far more collaborative and less disruptive to the entire effort. The traditional approach of publishing a *paper* is popular because there is a sense of closure, completion, permanence, and professionalism in the finished document. In a virtual environment the mutually agreed upon goal is to collectively create a high-quality final report, and sharing information electronically is the medium or conduit that enables this teamwork.

Many companies think that technology is the solution to workflow or productivity problems. For example, a company purchases a turnkey system that is supposed to solve a series of problems, one of which is to make the company more productive. The system is installed, the staff begins using it, and productivity raises a little but not to management's expectations. Technology is more a part, an ingredient in an overall solution; it will not solve employee work habit problems, workflow processes that are broken or need revision, or turn around low morale. In a virtual environment, technology is critical to supporting productivity efforts, but it is a tool that enables productivity; it is not the productivity tool. Internal organizational issues will still be internal organizational issues regardless of additional technologies implemented.

Keeping technology in its proper perspective of enabler, there are many tools available that enable file transfer, scanning of images and database access, and information sharing across a network. Wireless communications and worldwide data networks make access ubiquitous. Multimedia communications and presentations provide the media that supports everything from ASCII to full-motion 3-D graphics and video. The challenge is to design processes that utilize the full potential of existing technologies and can scale into new technologies as they emerge and are needed.

Processes of the virtual operation are not so far removed from traditional communications processes. In order to design a work process model and make significant positive impact on organizational performance, the process should have certain characteristics. It should include as much information from as many sources as possible and focus on the communication capabilities. Processes that have high information content can easily be transmitted through the network electronically within and across organizations. Processes should be developed with distributed and cross-functional resources in mind. They should require information to be widely distributed and in a format that is easily understood, inside and outside the core organization. The processes should be open to change and revision as required; they should not be stagnant.

Managing ongoing change is often the most visible feature of virtual operations. Processes that define in detail highly stable, extended, complex operations may mask the benefits of virtual operations. Processes that qualify as complex are composed of sub-processes that should be available to view and that can often be performed simultaneously. A dependency model that shows a high level of process flow can allow for virtual operations to be easily viewed. Drilling into the details highlights individual areas of responsibility, such as areas that work in parallel to one another. An example of this might be the aerospace contractor who staffs and manages a project support office for a major initiative.

An Aerospace Contractor

This aerospace contractor was under pressure from the federal government to eliminate cost overruns in an ongoing missile program. The contractor decided to reengineer existing processes in hopes of bringing the performance in line with these government expectations. At the same time, the organization hoped to gain insight regarding investing in technology and thereby achieve a better return on existing technology. Following are the steps that the company took.

Step One. A cross-functional team with representatives from executive, line, and supervisory management reviewed various processes to determine in which ones improvement could be made to dramatically reduce overruns. The team used traditional systems analysis methods to identify where wasted effort was taking place and finally settled on document review and the release process as candidates for redesign. *Review and release* is the formal process by which all project documents, including specifications, drawings, and change orders, are validated, verified, accepted, and officially released for implementation. The team found that most of this work was conducted via paper communications and little, if any, was done utilizing an electronic communications format.

In any system development effort, whether the system in question is a product, a service, or an organization, the proper and required document generation is complex, time consuming, and expensive. When late or erroneous information is released, it often results in later repercussions that incur costs in time and resources. The team chose review and release because it was a key area that could dramatically reduce project cycle times and costs. Team members decided to begin with one type of review and release and then apply the learning to similar processes in this area. In this way they could achieve an immediate benefit from the redesign and a more strategic value gained from a wider application of this knowledge.

In this case, the process chosen was the engineering change orders, the activity that managed significant changes to key documents relating to the complex systems being built, such as the component, the missile, and the aircraft. The process included activities ranging from the detection of the cause for change to dissemination of the information. Describing the change to the right people, negotiating support, conducting formal decisions, gaining approval, and releasing final documents was the process chosen for change. The process to replace was very paper oriented, face-to-face intensive, and highly structured. This was an issue because the information involved, until final approval, was very tentative and flexible. To constantly and repeatedly print, publish, distribute, edit, and revise documents took enormous support and time. Often key people were off-site on other assignments around the world when their competencies were needed. The face-to-face meetings generated huge costs in time and dollars to bring all necessary resources together for meetings. Scheduling and travel were terrible, and often stakeholders missed important parts of the meetings because of prior commitments; other times meetings needed to be rescheduled or were held without key participants. The existing process consumed time and resources, which often resulted in flawed decisions because of the inability to sustain communication among all of the necessary participants. At the same time, the engineering change orders process had all the elements for redesign, including: information and communication issues, distributed resource-required participation, and competency-based project work, involving experts and extremely complex sub-processes that could be performed simultaneously if reviewed.

Having decided on the processes to target, management empowered an experienced virtual project team to develop a proposal that would reduce cycle time through reengineering these processes. The new processes needed to take advantage of existing technologies whenever possible, and if new technologies were required, they needed to be quickly identified and economically implemented.

Step Two. Developing the new virtual processes was the goal. The team identified that the major drivers of time and cost were the current performance of engineering change orders process tasks. It developed new virtual processes that would avoid the pitfalls of the current environment. Detection of these pitfalls was the prime cause of the change; the challenge was to raise the visibility of the problem and find immediate solutions. If a structural engineer realized that the current landing gear was too weak to handle new payload configurations, he had to be able to note the problem and fix it without impacting the schedule or budget. It might mean convening a team of experts in materials, stress management, and business planning who could assess the situation and offer suggestions for resolution.

Continuous input from this solution team was needed. This team would be distributed throughout the world; therefore, the challenge would be to provide an accessible electronic mechanism for review, dialogue, and communication. Information sharing was important for all of the product and process participants who had an interest in the change and the effects on the rest of the systems. Steadier landing gear might be proposed but that could affect other aspects of the product, such as fuel consumption or cargo space. Those responsible for these other areas needed to be aware of the suggested resolutions to quickly identify any impacts from these ideas.

Making all relevant information available to all potential stakeholders and reviewers was essential. Not knowing everyone who might be affected, wide access to information had to be provided. There was no time to wait for uninformed participants to accidentally discover the change and the possible impact on their areas of expertise. Also, access to deliberations, negotiations, and closure was required, and the final approved changes needed to be shared with all participants, regardless of location or area of focus.

The final engineering change orders processes took advantage of E-mail, computer-to-computer communications, and audio conferencing as major communication tools. The team considered what improvements were possible by making moderate investments in technology. It used more structured methodologies, utilizing as many existing technologies as possible. Team members used E-mail distribution lists to announce the need for any engineering changes and to convene a review process. All milestones and their status in the review process were communicated via E-mail as well. They also set up a computer-to-computer conference for online changes, one that was accessible via the Internet or Telnet through a high-speed 800 number dial-up line. Communications included the posting of relevant documents, as well as dialogue about defects and problems, input from participants who were affected by the changes, and the final decisions. They held professionally facilitated audio conferences for issue resolution; all documentation relating to these conferences was sent ahead to ensure that all participants were ready. There were post-meeting minutes with issues, resolutions, and action items for all participants, especially for those who could not attend the conference. There was also a later face-to-face meeting for approval, sign off, and relationship or team building that proved extremely helpful.

Step Three. After implementing these new processes the engineering change orders project team found significant and interesting improvements. For example, it found dramatic reductions in the time needed to process changes, a result of an acceleration of document development; support for continuous communications; elimination of travel time productivity loss; and the elimination of the need to physically assemble participants to handle crises. There was an increased awareness of quality decision-making, as well. With all project participants having access to documents, problems, and solutions, the entire project effort was better understood, and there were less problems later. Continuous communications between participants caused a new occurrence called the *phantom reviewer*, a collaborative review with various points of view for continuous online revisions and conclusions. Finally, there was a dramatic reduction in costs; unproductive time and poor quality were identified as the major cost drivers. Accelerating the process and delivering the right decisions saved rework for present and later resources.

It is clear from this situation that the most critical, as well as the most strategic, step in virtual operations or virtual project management is to keep the lines of communication open to all participants and with the overall management team. Decisions must be communicated to all in a timely manner. A virtual operation means that information is both valued and shared; this includes sharing both the good and the bad news. In the absence of a structured communications process, fear and misinformation can persist, thereby increasing uncertainty and lowering morale and quality. By leading the corporation in the direction it should be going, the virtual project task force keeps things on track by monitoring the progress toward the goal, thus avoiding later surprises to the organization. The virtual project task force is proactive and ahead of changes; it sets the expectations, facilitates natural transitions, and enables the organization to assimilate any changes. It is critical to evaluate where the organization is in time to reduce the risk of an underestimation of capabilities and the resource drain that could occur as a result.

Management Resource Group

The Management Resource Group (MRG), a New England consulting firm, assists top executives with identifying management leadership attributes and behaviors needed to transition their organizations. The company saw an opportunity to develop a virtual relationship with another organization located in Canada. In reviewing existing relationships, processes, and technologies, it became clear that a change was necessary in how MRG worked with its alliance partners. The company found that planning was cursory, and teams expected the unexpected; communication was random and did not provide the support needed; and there was no clarity of vision or processes. Therefore, it made the most sense to initiate a project team to address virtual operations in these areas. MRG compiled existing information of exactly how each area functioned, what needed to be worked on in each area, which areas could be transitioned, and in what timeframe. It also identified problem areas that could cause difficulties later, as well as the likely areas for virtual operations, thereby addressing two issues at the same time.

Management Resource Group spent quite a lot of time in the planning stage of the change life cycle. It did a cursory planning session to identify both the expected and the unexpected results and realized that the culture needed to change. The realization allowed the company to identify many of the potential pitfalls. However, it could not plan for unexpected issues that might surface. It did, though, address how unexpected issues might be solved, in what timeframe, and how these resolutions would be communicated.

The company realized that focus needed to center on more frequent communications and a better overall way of communicating. All of this information became the baseline for operations. MRG also needed to revamp its internal processes, review and update employee competencies, and upgrade or install new technologies in order to transition into virtual operations.

The findings of MRG are not surprising; most companies rely on ad hoc meetings and implied processes. Management Resource Group (MRG) realized that the entire organization needed to be changed and refocused its efforts in order to become a more virtual operation and employ global project teams. The result of this preliminary research was vital in assisting MRG in planning its transition, as well as managing the transition task forces. The company is currently in the midst of a successful transition process.

Successful Transitioning

Transitioning to virtual operations is usually a result of a directive from executive management that is clearly related to corporate vision. There is a planned, clear direction for the corporation that is both understandable and well communicated. The up-front planning must include both the benefits and the risks, as well as provide some incentives for staff to *buy into* the vision. It is critical to identify and communicate the success factors so that everyone begins with the same frame of reference. Normally, sharing critical company information with the entire organization gives everyone an opportunity to understand and evaluate the ideas and success factors. This is usually a very positive element necessary for a successful cultural transition throughout the enterprise.

In a transition, there are some areas that must be addressed. It is essential to identify appropriate delivery mechanisms and in what context they are used, such as face-to-face meetings, E-mail, voice mail, bulletin boards, newsletters, and Internet and intranet access to information and communications. Virtual operations implementation is better left to a team to plan and staff, although there should be participation from cross-functional groups to better represent the entire enterprise. The virtual project team needs to be a flexible driver in both the transitional planning and ongoing communications. The planning and design documents should be available real time to all members of the team and to others that may see the value in staying updated on the implementation. In addition, the transition team should be able to work on this project and its own project work simultaneously; this need not be a full-time assignment.

In determining an organization's viability to transition to virtual operations, an organizational assessment needs to be conducted. Even if this assessment proves that the transition would be beneficial, there are always barriers that must be overcome in order for any cultural change to be complete. While the virtual processes seem obvious improvements over the rational ones, there are always barriers to implementing and sustaining virtual work. It is important to begin by creating an environment in which people will understand and be comfortable with the concept of a virtual workplace. Many employees are reluctant to use electronic infrastructures to do their work, which may be highly communicative, knowledge intensive, and socially focused. They communicate better face to face, enjoy less persuading over the phone, are resistant to widespread electronic information sharing, and do not have a sensitivity for the planning and formality necessary to make virtual processes work.

Also, it has often been found that using distributed resources is a problem when the normal convention is to have all resources physically co-located. When the link to resources is electronic, many *hands-on* managers feel a loss of control. Formal information sharing is difficult at best in traditional organizations, and introducing an electronic means to communicate might be seen as threatening, especially if outsider organizations and potential competitors are included. The best way to approach these barriers is to encourage people who perform the processes to be part of the redesign effort; make the goals and advantages visible; train people in virtual operations and teaming; and reward those who experiment with the new virtual processes. In the case of reluctant management—regarding how they will *control* employees they cannot see—how they manage employees that can be seen is the question that needs to be asked.

It is also necessary to identify and address areas that might prove detrimental when changing an organization into a virtual corporation. There are many questions to ask—and answers evaluated. Some examples follow.

Do people work well together today? Do they resist taking direction from outside their established chain of command? Is turf protection a major cultural factor? Are people compensated according to the number of employees that they manage?

Are there pockets of knowledge that might feel threatened and therefore try to sabotage change? Can the project team members handle high-profile and high-performance visibility and accountability? Is there a cultural bias of *not invented here* or it's *not the company way*? Is there a risk of sabotage? Are there any groups that would resort to this to save their *empires*?

Has anyone in any group ever worked on a virtual team before? If yes, how has it operated? How are project team members selected? Is open communication practiced? If so, how? How do you prepare organizations, team members, and managers for changes? Are there rigid political relationships that could influence the success or failure of this transition? Are there any inhibitors to team activity, such as people who never perform well on a team? Is there any negative history with an external provider that could pose problems, distrust, or friction? Are there language barriers? If so, how do you overcome these today?

Is the technology integrated; are there LANs, WANs, and intranets, or are major changes necessary? Does the existing infrastructure need to be upgraded or replaced? Is the internal LAN network adequate? Can it accommodate bandwidth and access demands of the future? Is the external WAN network set up for remote access? Is it global? Is adequate security in place? If not, what are the reasons for not allowing remote access?

Are there resource issues that could compromise the success of the change? What changes in work processes and management systems are needed in order to ensure the success of the teams? How open is the enterprise to change?

Of course there are more considerations; these are provided to help begin the thought processes needed to evaluate the barriers to change.

With the introduction of technology-enabling systems, information overload may become a problem. Information overload may inhibit the success and productivity of individuals and cause problems in technology-based communications solutions. Couple this with barriers to change that often cause stress, and projects and cultural transitions could be defeated!

Surmounting Barriers

Identifying and managing barriers is a skill unto itself. There are ways to address embedded reluctance to change. Educating and empowering leaders to make employees aware of the corporate and personal benefits of virtual processes, as well as how barriers and stress can be negative experiences for them, is very helpful. Providing proactive situational learning in networking processes and technologies is important. This will foster collaboration and assist in barrier confrontation in a non-threatening way. Trying to transition to a paperless environment or trying to reduce travel are lofty goals that are often misunderstood, and their messages may be poorly communicated. Explaining the value to the corporation of working in this new way is the message that often is implied rather than communicated. Seeking innovative ways of using electronic communications to keep the teams constantly informed is critical as the speed of communications increases. The work-life balance has become a corporate motto that is a means for informing employees of potentially stressful situations. Once informed, they may work through the stress in a better way; perhaps they will telecommute one day a week and reduce stress while being more productive.

Assessing the current culture and how people work is critical to the success of transitioning to virtual operations. Where and how do employees get their information? Do they have ad hoc meetings with one another at the coffee machine? How does this translate when they are no longer in the same building? Do they rely on subordinates to communicate or give updates? How will they do this when their staff is virtual? Are there formal or informal communication techniques? Both techniques probably exist, but how will they exist in the new culture? Are employees empowered to assume responsibility and make decisions; if so, to what extent? How is feedback accepted? Are people open to feedback, or do they feel threatened? How can a corporation ensure that everyone gets all information about the transition and does not feel left out? What needs to happen at each stage of implementation to make sure the transition proceeds smoothly?

All of these questions must be addressed and built into a strategy for the transition.

Employees need to understand the drivers that are causing the organization to make this cultural change. What are the existing programs that would be affected by a virtual operation? There are always hidden agendas or masked drivers that appear at the worst time. It is important to understand the entire organization and flush out these agendas, address them, and proceed.

Is the organization ready to develop corporate alliances based on competency, or are friendships or politics too deeply embedded? If so, there needs to be a strategy developed to assist in resolving this barrier. Are there established values, histories, or expectations for virtual activities? These might have originated with someone's fear that was then communicated to others. Does the company have published policies (telecommute program, external access security, and so on) that will be available during this transition? It is unwise to begin a transition of this kind without involving the human resources area in the plans and making formal published policies available. Are formal training programs provided to prepare individuals for virtual activities, and do they include virtual teaming? Does the training include skills needed for virtual team operations? Is it designed for project managers, team members, and/or management?

Which term does your organization use to identify outside resources: vendor, supplier, outsource provider, partner, consultant, contractor, or any or all of the above? Are outside resources allowed controlled access to your information network, E-mail, or documentation? If not, this needs to be considered if partnering is part of the virtual project management plans. Are there processes in place for some partners to have full network and information system access or intranet access? Do outside resources participate in meetings, design sessions, customer service activities, reviews, or training? How do outside contributors participate in the decision process? How are interactions with outside contributors conducted? Are they considered part of the communications channel and receive memos and documentation or participate in face-to-face meetings? Can they receive information through an electronic medium?

Do cross-functional or virtual teams exist in your organization today? If they currently exist, it is helpful to review their success to better understand what may need to be done to improve them or to highlight them as prototypes for the future. If there have been virtual teams, how was their success measured? Are there existing structures, practices, and processes in place? Are they current? Do they need review and revision to better fit into the new virtual operation?

Are project status reports published at various times and at the conclusion of projects? What level sees these reports, and how is this information shared with upper levels of management? If reports are shared, what communications mechanism is used? Does the corporation have a group that audits projects? If not, this should be put into place to better understand the changes within a virtual organization. Is team performance rewarded? Is project conclusion acknowledged? How does the organization identify and value results and contributions? Is there focus on: output measured by quality or quantity, contribution to process, planned or ad hoc commitment to quality as a goal, individual or team accomplishments, commitment to improved process or product development, adapting to changing environments or processes, or interpersonal communication skills? Are interactions outside the organization valued?

Do all levels of the organization participate in a reward or recognition process? Are there formal standards for measuring team performance? Are there incentives for experienced team leaders to mentor less-experienced leaders? Team participation must be encouraged and rewarded in order for virtual operations, and subsequently virtual project teams, to be successful. This will form the underlying infrastructure for this virtual organization.

Committing to the Change

Let's jump ahead a bit and assume that a virtual project has been identified. The team members have been identified, their time has been negotiated, and they are ready to begin. All members are required to meet for a face-to-face kickoff meeting so that there will be recognition of each team member and his project contribution. The communications and reporting strategies for the project are identified during this kickoff meeting. The communications and reporting strategies address how often the entire team will meet face to face, how often the project will be statused, how individuals will communicate with one another (voice mail, E-mail, groupware, and so on), and how issues, problems, and unforeseen occurrences will be addressed.

This kickoff meeting sets the tone and spirit of the entire project team; it gains agreement for the reporting and communications expectations that

Table 4. Delivery Systems

Pushing	Pulling
Unfiltered E-mail	Bulletin boards
Voice mail	Document control
Phone calls	Internets/intranets
Face to face	Web pages
Faxes	Groupware, E-mail

do not need to be revisited at a later time. This step is critical in a virtual project because resources may be located around the world, and these fundamental processes must be in place early. These preliminary planning activities must successfully occur for the team to better communicate and understand the dependencies created by task work. Once the team members have a clear understanding of the frequency of meetings, meetings can be held via audio conferences or videoconferences with documentation sent ahead of time. This method eliminates the need for resources to be co-located so that they can be wherever necessary for them to be most effective. The most difficult part of conducting an audio conference or videoconference is scheduling worldwide, as someone will invariably be up at an awfully early or late time.

There are many examples of companies that use virtual project teams and virtual project resources. In some areas, in order to secure the best resources, companies are required to be as flexible as possible concerning resource location. It is often more cost effective and productive to have virtual project teams. The need for a specific resource talent can be better specified as to when that talent is actually required, rather than keeping the resource on the payroll. In addition, industry experts often are working on their own, focused on multiple projects that require their specific talents. A virtual team member is often virtual in many projects. The need for specific resources at varying stages of a project is normal project staffing and assignment identification. Often when resources are needed and supplied from organizations or groups outside the project's own area, these resources will devote a percentage of their time to this project.

Tracking the amount of time spent on a project and the impact of this on a task's duration is critical in managing these resources. Often, the resources are under the management of others, and the project manager has little influence over ensuring that resources perform to set standards.

Many companies are considering or using a different model. They are dedicating resources to a project, or project support resources, for the time their specific skills are needed. It is a similar model except that these resources carry no other projects at the time when they are needed; they are free to devote their time to one project and move to the next when they are needed. This model requires coordinated project, task, and resource tracking to ensure resource availability.

Virtual projects require more planning and communication—often over-communication—in order to be successful. This means that information may need to be sent in many ways: E-mail, voice mail, and posting on project bulletin boards. Resources need to know the progress and pitfalls that are occurring in real time, and open, continual communication is the only way to ensure that they feel connected. A virtual project team member may be an outsourced resource, or he may be an internal skilled resource working on a part of the project that may be produced by another company. The basics of managing the team are the same except that the chances of running into one another in a common place have been eliminated completely. The context has changed.

The overwhelming need for communication technology is never more visible than in this type of team. The participants not only are dispersed, but the communications tools they use within their companies may not be linked nor even made by the same manufacturer. An example of this is in how companies use their PBXs or phone systems. In one company with an internal distributed team, four- or five-digit dialing, group messaging, and E-mail systems often can accommodate the distance. In a totally virtual team, these communications methods and technologies are very different. There is no longer the capability to use one voice mail system for a distribution list. Dissimilar voice mail systems do not allow for messaging between one another; the only way to do this is with electronic mail. Everyone sees the same message, but often enclosures do not transfer well. This virtual project team brings with it many communications challenges.

Table 5. Urgency of Communications

High	Low

Important and urgent
    Example: An activity is delaying a project, and the deadlines are at risk.
	Important but not urgent
	    Example: A meeting is being scheduled next week, and materials must be prepared.

Urgent but not important
    Examples: phone calls
	Neither urgent nor important
	    Examples: reading faxes, drop-in visitors, some E-mail, conference materials, magazines

---

Project Manager/Project Leader

As the project manager of a virtual team, extra discipline is required in order to set the pace and the standards for team. In team communications, for example, she must ensure that all members feel important, have all communications and access to documentation necessary, and are kept informed of all new occurrences. The team is dependent on the project manager for keeping the project on track, identifying issues, and assisting in their resolution. Specific meeting times, deliverables, communication strategies, and reports and issues format must be designed, shared, and communicated by the project manager. Holding team members accountable is the only way to ensure that a virtual project team completes the project on time and on budget and thus creates a positive experience for all.

The trend for companies is toward more dispersed project resources from inside and outside the basic structure of the company. The challenge for participants and project managers is to ensure that all members have a positive experience and find the virtual project team a desirable alternative. This seems to be the way that the fast-paced world is headed. Early adapters must decide if they are right for this type of project, structure, and process.

Project leaders need to be competent in their specialties, techniques, and technical support requirements for virtual operations and virtual team leadership. Their competencies lie in how well the following questions are answered.

How do project managers acquire these competencies? Do these leaders have authority over team members within the scope of the project? Do the team members know who is directly responsible for their work activities? Are there limits on open access to project information? Can everyone who needs it access information?

How do the organization and the team respond to crisis? Are there different reactions, depending on the crisis? Does the project manager have much decision-making responsibility? Who has final decision-making authority on a project? Are team decisions made by individuals, by special interest groups, or by consensus?

The role of the project manager for virtual project management is different from that for a co-located project team. The basic project management skills must be in place, but flexibility and communications skills must be highly developed. The project manager is the glue in a virtual project more than was ever imagined. If he does not promote communications and collaboration, it is likely that the team will not pick this up on its own. The project manager and communications are almost synonymous. Setting expectations is critical in any communications, but it becomes even more vital when distance adds another dimension to the team. Prioritizing communications is one technique that can help in ensuring that everyone is informed. The ways to prioritize, and their delivery systems, are different. The project manager may use any and all of the delivery systems presented in Table 4 as the project progresses. Each has its purpose and, of course, the more sophisticated it is, the more work it requires for setting up and using. In addition to the type of delivery needed for communications is the urgency and response of the communications. In our virtual communications, we often forget the human things that face-to-face communications takes for granted.

What Do We Take for Granted?

We take the frequency of face-to-face communications for granted when we are located in the same building or on the same campus. It is easy to forget that the acknowledgments we receive through body language when speaking real time with one another are not visible when using other forms of communications. It is no longer common to have informal information exchanges; every exchange with virtual team members is either not real time or is scheduled. This often inhibits the casual sharing of thoughts as we come up with ideas unless effort is made to formally communicate these.

Another forgotten area has to do with the *out-of-mind* resources that work at a distance. They are often overlooked in communications, as well as in the control of resources, their time, and work habits. It is very important to remember these out-of-mind resources and their needs for communication.

Context is another area to consider. How do we communicate with one another when we are looking at each other? These unconscious movements or assumptions do not translate electronically. Consider, for example, when you're on the phone: How often do you shake your head in agreement? Assume the other person knows you are smiling? Assume the other person knows you are not in agreement? Work on the computer and only half listen? Commit to something and then forget the commitment? When using E-mail, do you ever: Speak in an angry voice? Write in all capital letters? Say things you would never say in person? Often send things with typographical errors or misspellings? Not acknowledge receipt of E-mail? Forget to check or send E-mail?

What is context, and why bother? How you communicate—your expressions and mannerisms—is what constitutes context. Context is closing the loop on questions and issues, ensuring availability and concern. Consider how you are relating context when you are on the phone, in a video or audio conference, leaving voice mail (brief or lengthy), developing E-mail, preparing materials for faxing, or preparing materials for FedEx or the United States Postal Service. All of these are examples of thinking about context in a non-face-to-face setting. *Think of how you would communicate in a design review or technical or status meeting if the team was globally dispersed. Consider the best way to communicate positive or negative feedback. Always ask yourself how you would feel receiving this information before choosing a medium.*

Soliciting or providing technical information might be one easy way for using E-mail, as the technical information is often written anyway, and this would be one of the best ways of sharing this type of information. Coaching or teaching might provide a variety of ways to share that would work for communications. Assigning work might be done with a combination of a phone call and then E-mail to send any written instructions of documentation. Conducting a performance review or a brainstorming session, however, seems to need person-to-person real-time communications. The performance review is a personal thing that requires personal attention. A brainstorming session, although available through software, is conducted more effectively when all participants can see the results of the sessions written on a white board. Either a face-to-face meeting or videoconferencing would work for this communications methodology.

Basic questions to continue asking yourself include the following: How would you ensure communications were effective? How would you provide the right medium for the message? How would you prioritize the communications? What would you do to change the communications if the method was ineffective? How open are you to changing your chosen method of communications?

There are several keys to successful distributed teams. Formal procedures and processes are essential to set and maintain expectations. Well-integrated tools are necessary and quite helpful to a distributed team. Obtaining an executive sponsor who understands the value and difficulty of distributed teams is critical.

If services are what your team focuses on, are there defined life cycles for service, and are there documented rollout strategies? How you measure project and team effectiveness; having critical success factors is important in knowing whether or not you and your team have succeeded.

Assessing your communications methods should be done periodically to ensure that they are not limited to direct or ambiguous communications. Reliable and consistent communications are also essential, especially if communications are conducted at a distance. There are many considerations, including context or how communications is done, the medium or form communications take, processes that the team knows and shares, and the reliability of whatever communications medium is chosen. Communications is not trivial; it can be a showstopper if not addressed and resolved.

Distributed teams are composed of people working in the same organization but in different locations. This may include team members from other floors, buildings, states, or countries. They may work from an office at times, from home, or on the road. The fact that they are not co-located is the differentiating factor. A variation on this is the distributed cross-functional team in which people from different organizations of the same company work together on a project. They may be in the same building, but they may not be, just as well. One constant in distributed, virtual teams is that the greater the distance between the team members the less real-time communications occurs. Using the messaging capability of technologies accomplishes the communication link, and the response occurs when it is convenient for the team member. Difficulty in scheduling occurs quite often in virtual teams, as the greater the distance from one another the more potential for time-zone intrusion. If there is a nine-hour difference between team members, then scheduling a real-time conference call will surely inconvenience at least one of the members.

Corporate Examples

There are many examples of virtual, global teams. One example is Boston's First Community Bank (FCB), which has a partnership with Overseas Chinese Credit Guarantee Fund in Taiwan. There are team members from both companies on a virtual project to offer funds overseas. The team members also include Chinese community groups in Boston and representatives from the Taiwanese government. This team has to address the same issues of distance and communications as does any other virtual team, but it has the added issues of culture and language. Another example is Eastman Kodak, which has virtual teams as high as the executive level in the organization. Eastman Kodak has presidents in each of its manufacturing areas, and these presidents have formed their own virtual teams to share information, resolve issues, and address global opportunities.

The keys to any project's success, and especially to a virtual team's success, are the sponsor, mission, and objectives. A virtual team needs to know who the sponsor is and what her vision is for the project's completion. The team would then develop a scope of the project and forward it to the sponsor to ensure it met with her expectations. The goals would then be developed into actual deliverables, with roles and responsibilities identified, to ensure team member understanding. Without the sponsor and mission, the virtual project team could head in a direction that is not in alignment with the organizational objectives. Virtual projects especially need this foundation because they are often quite removed from the sponsoring location and the *seat of power* in the organization.

Virtual teams are often made up of alliance partners, with team members and deliverables coming from different companies. NCR has projects with its own development teams in California, South Carolina, and Illinois in the United States (U.S.) with complementary development groups in India and China. There are also database development teams in Southern

California, communications software teams in New Jersey (U.S.), marketing and administration in Ohio (U.S.), and manufacturing in Southern California and Ireland. Representatives from each of these areas are on a virtual project team that has alliance partner participation from Intel, EMC, Symbios Login, Informix, and Microsoft. These alliance partners have team members throughout the United States.

The team uses every possible means of technology and electronic communications available. It even modified traditional voice mail systems to allow for subgroup messaging so that the entire team could be messaged at the same time, as well as forward messages to one another easily. Members use room videoconferencing when the entire team needs to get together and desktop videoconferencing when smaller, sub-teams need to communicate via computer-to-computer conferencing. Other forms of communication include E-mail with enclosures for collaboration, an online project management system for task and milestone tracking, and a Web homepage for links to one another's databases. One reason this virtual team is successful is because of its utilization of communications technologies and its overall commitment to team communications.

5

Connectivity

The Need for Stable Networking Infrastructures and Tools

Connectivity, in this context, means being attached, having the ability via networking to access information from another source. This means that networks deliver more importance and have more value than in previous times. Today's networking infrastructure must be able to provide users with access to whatever systems they require; these systems gather, hold, and transport the information needed to do the work. Information must be available to resources wherever they work, whenever they need it, and in a form that is useful to them. As the speed of computing increases, so does the expectation for access and document turnaround time. Connectivity is the driver that enables almost instantaneous communications regardless of location or time zone.

Today public and private network facilities connect globally; communication within a company or between multiple companies is possible for voice as well as for data communications. A hybrid network, one consisting of many pieces of equipment and transport operated by a variety of companies, may connect a board of directors located around the world, utilizing audio-conferencing technology. One director may be using a cellular phone in a car; another, a telephone in an office; and another, on an airplane. The device and location of the participants is not an issue any longer—we can reach people wherever they happen to be.

This type of multidevice, multilocation communication is commonplace in a virtual corporation. The cornerstone of virtual operations is ubiquitous connectivity. Once connections are made, information must flow to whoever needs it at a time when it is needed. Within a corporate network, interoperability is assumed; there is the ability to communicate with one another easily. Virtual operations seamlessly link unrelated resources that are connected to different networks or services. There is no guarantee that a virtual project team made up of members from different corporations will have a problem-free information exchange. Problem-free communications is dependent on a stable network infrastructure. In a virtual environment the information infrastructure must work all of the time, every time; there is often no fallback and no sympathy for lack of connectivity. A well-managed infrastructure provides project participants with information access and enables them to anticipate and measure the team interaction, instead of having to think about the network capability. This is why many virtual teams use the Internet for their global communications.

The Internet, a revolutionary transport, external to any business, has changed the way people communicate in a very short time. This backbone network has been around for a long time, used by the military and universities for private communications. The recent opening of the Internet to all computer users has been the phenomenon that has changed global communications as dramatically as telephone access did many years ago. About three years ago access became more available, and E-mail addresses and host sites began to grow. Today, individual Web pages and chat rooms have opened the door to interactive communications worldwide.

Marshall McLuhan popularized the term *global village*. Some Internet service providers (ISPs) try to give the impression that the Internet is a village. The Internet is not a global village, because in a village everyone knows everyone else and often what they are doing as well. The Internet is more like a large *global city* where people co-exist and share but generally do not know all of the inhabitants. Although with new software developments, ISPs and others can gather quite a lot of information about Internet users. The Internet is more like a vast number of separate communities with separate interests, linked together at will. Like a city, the Internet brings many cultures and communities into close proximity with one another so that they can learn and share from one another. The Internet has an immense storehouse and diversity of information sources where members do not meet physically but can have a close rapport socially. One can *surf* the net, meet people, share information, and manage projects through electronic means. It is a new and unique way of communicating at a distance.

The intranet, an in-house repository of information similar to the Internet, is another tool that resides within corporations as an internal nervous system for information. The intranet can link departments, customers, agents, and affiliate corporations worldwide just by being the central point for storing reusable documentation. Some groups build a shared intranet for collective use with departmental Web pages linked to supporting documentation. Hewlett-Packard, for example, operates an internal board called a *software vending machine*, providing a method for software developers to check for best practices prior to writing new code. They also have department Web pages, project Web pages for group access, and external access to the Internet for research. The new Hollywood studio, DreamWorks, started by Steven Spielberg, has an organizational intranet used to track animation objects and the coordination of scenes shot at different locations. By providing access to developers for content animation and sound, the studio is better able to get projects completed by people in different locations.

Bulletin boards, associated with Web-based or workgroup applications, offer still other ways for dispersed staff and teams to communicate. Bulletin boards are an electronic place for posting messages that can be read worldwide; actually anybody with a computer can set one up or access existing ones. Corporate intranets employ similar boards to communicate among employees or to provide databases for corporate functions. There are many types of bulletin boards, such as the following:

• Open boards: Anyone can connect to the board and say anything about its subject matter. There is no attempt to supervise the board's content. These are often found at ISP locations.

• Controlled discussion boards: A systems operator runs this board, issues announcements, and controls the subject matter. This is often found within a company's intranet.

• Electronic publications: This board is run like a magazine with editorial control but with more flexibility than a paper magazine. It allows for submission of articles that are published on the board if they meet certain requirements.

• Boards with heavily supervised content: A system operator seeks academic and responsible behavior and reviews the content and the quality of the contents. These are often found in universities with specific standards and controls.

- Information databases: This board makes available a vast amount of information, usually updated by board users themselves. This could be a board used by a virtual project team with a specific function and audience. All of these boards provide a central place for information sharing and interactive communications.

A virtual corporation can use many different types of highways, networks, and communications connectivity tools in order to make information and collaboration available. The Internet is readily accessible worldwide and has an easy end-user interface. A browser and access to the Internet are the only real requirements for sharing Internet information. The intranet, a private version of the Internet, uses similar software browser technology, but it uses workgroup software as well. Today's corporate networks are designed for fast, two-way response and are often built for videoconferencing and multimedia demands, as well. VISA International, for example, has a private fiber network for handling extremely high-transmission volumes, files with significant bandwidth. Other companies use private high-speed circuits between locations when heavy traffic patterns or videoconferencing and multimedia are required. Some medical clinics have leased lines to major hospitals for remote examinations; this is becoming a focus for collaborative, distributed work teams. Corporate private networks often handle airline reservations for airlines around the world or electronic funds transfer for banks; these are all transparent to the corporations that use them. Integrated services digital network circuits (ISDN), with 2-56K channels, allow interaction with graphic images for faster response time and higher-quality transmissions. Frame-relay networks link corporate locations at bandwidth on-demand megabit speeds for video interaction or high-capacity data transmission. Some regional operating companies are beginning to offer digital subscriber line (DSL) access, utilizing existing copper wire, into the building for high-speed access to the Internet. The Internet linked to cable television, via cable modems, is a potentially powerful transmission medium; this is in trial across the United States. It is clear that the Internet and information availability is in demand. Internet service providers (ISPs) are gaining new customers daily as more and more companies and individual users feel a need to access or share information globally. The Internet certainly has added tremendously to virtual project team and distributed work force communication.

The Internet as a Virtual Tool for Communication

These days the business use of the Internet has grown tremendously. Many companies have direct gateway links from their LANs to the Internet for employees to search for information whenever they need to. There is often even after-hour access through the company gateway for the employee who needs to work in the evening or on weekends. Companies that haven't implemented this access often think of it as wasteful, implying that the employee will play instead of work. That may be the case in the beginning because it is new, but most employees use the access for research and staying ahead of competition. There are many business uses of the Internet for sales and marketing, as it can be searched for new markets and online products; there are electronic shopping malls that offer an incredible variety of products; Wal-Mart is one of them. There is access to online catalogs, with changing processes, features, and details, offering constantly updated information for whatever the business or personal need; this allows for online order-taking directly to the manufacturer or distributor. The Internet has proven to be a very inexpensive communication tool with potential for customers worldwide.

One of the most popular business uses is the electronic distribution of software, upgrades, *fixes* to known problems, business publications, and music. These Web sites allow the employee to find whatever is needed to do work. The Internet, in its own way, provides an open communications channel for inter-business communications. Some Web sites have online chat sessions with help desk personnel; others have a direct phone link into a *live* help-desk person for real-time communications. Yes, voice over the Internet is becoming quite popular.

From a sales and marketing perspective, the Internet could allow customers to continuously purchase goods without replacing orders; there could be an automatic order process, thereby allowing customers the ability to state when and how much to ship and at what time of the month.

The Internet obviously allows corporations to be in constant contact with more customers. Web sites offer an interactive form of advertising: customizable and on demand to the customer. There is the ability to better target consumers, as their order information is captured digitally, allowing for micromarketing linked to individual or corporate requirements, tastes, and profiles. This digital ability allows for faster user feedback, product reviews, problem information, suggestions, and concerns. The data accumulated assists in market research and knowledge of related products; this could allow for cross selling of products and services. It also enables continuous dealer forecasting, worldwide facilities planning, more accurate production planning, and, in Wal-Mart and others' cases, reduced inventory and warehouse space that provides significant cost savings.

The Internet allows for online product design, as engineers can be located across the globe but can access the same information simultaneously. There is access to component availability and vendor information from anywhere allowing for good, timely product design decisions. Links to suppliers for joint design is a major advantage over sending drawings to one another for review and requirements. This ability facilitates the knowledge of potential low-cost facilities and resources in distant countries. The Internet provides the ability to link to design consultants and research facilities worldwide; it allows for remote access to knowledge, information, literature, and documentation searches; access to remote supercomputers; and collaboration with universities or other groups with shared interests.

In some corporations the awareness of global technical trends is critical to its success, as products and services depend on international markets. Customer support has come of age with use of the Internet. Online customer service or help desk support is in its youth and becoming more popular as competition for customers increases. Having online access allows for faster problem identification and resolution, direct access to expertise, and more satisfied customers. The frequently asked questions often assist customers in resolving the problem themselves or in knowing that the company is aware of the problem.

There is a communications tool that is important in customer as well as in virtual team communications. Customer, corporate, and team newsletters often supply information to the most appropriate people without having to seek out the right person. These newsletters allow for the interchange of product, division, and project knowledge, as well as product use, due dates, and expected completion or results. This way of supplying communication is called *push* because the recipient subscribes to this and is automatically sent information.

Manufacturing can also benefit from Internet access and presence. Often a corporation is seeking a supplier of specific goods and services. Using the Internet it could gather supplier information for better selection, identify low cost components from a variety of suppliers, have direct communication with a supplier, and be better able to make forecasts and track inventory.

For distributed teams in virtual corporations, often user-group discussions are important. These can be online sessions for specific attendees that address issues, topics, and events or provide the most recent status. This method of communications allows small, self-sufficient empowered teams with access to resources as needed. This is critical in virtual operations where external resources are utilized as required for specific tasks at varied times. This method of communications allows virtual project teams to span the globe and stay informed.

Project Management Infrastructure

Project management methodology and tools are critical for any virtual project team to be successful. Utilizing the Internet for access is one thing but seeing information in the right form and at the right time is equally as critical to the team's success. In order to ensure that virtual team members share information, another basic infrastructure must be in place: project management fundamentals. This infrastructure consists of project management planning and scheduling tools, communications strategy, workflow processes, and groupware tools.

Project management planning tools are those that allow for development of agreed upon strategies and processes. These could include how often teams meet—face to face and via conference technology, how often status information is conveyed, what resources are available to complete tasks, and when and what type of reporting is required at all levels involved with the project effort. Scheduling tools are applications such as Project Scheduler by Scitor, Microsoft Project by Microsoft, Primavera and Suretrak by Primavera, Timeline, AutoPlan, and many others. Their focus is primarily on identifying all tasks, deliverables, milestones, dependencies, and resources against a schedule in order for projects to be tracked and completed. The up-front planning and information input into one of these applications is critical for reporting, accurate tracking, and communications of project status and issues. The time necessary to develop and complete the actual project plan is often weeks in duration, but the long-term ability to view project status, task completion, and resource loading is worth the effort. Reports can be generated from these applications, informing the virtual team about status, delays, and successes, as well as cost and resource usage. Management and customers can be kept abreast of the project easily by viewing a report, sorted with appropriate information for specific needs, that will identify milestones and deliverables against a calendar (Gantt) to better set and manage ongoing expectations. When unforeseen delays occur, the project plan can show the impact of these delays on specific tasks and dependencies, as well as on the overall project. This allows for scenario development to brainstorm possible ways of resolving conflict and meeting expectations. These tools are helpful in communicating to both management and customers vital project information that may assist in decision-making.

Groupware, or collaborative computing, is a hot topic these days. The sales of groupware products doubled yearly; based on that, sales should be over $11 billion in 1997. Every thirty days almost one million new corporate E-mail boxes are installed. This figure does not include users of E-mail provided by Internet service providers (ISPs) like America Online (AOL), Compuserve, AT&T, MCI, Big Foot, Hot Mail, Juno, and so on. The groupware market sizzled with over sixty million users in 1996 and is estimated to have doubled again in 1997. Why is groupware a product of choice for collaborative virtual project teams? At present, there are over ten thousand—and growing daily—Internet newsgroups, 75,000 postings per day on typical online services, and nearly fifty new E-mail messages per day per typical employee. These products allow teams to gain communications, support, and information at levels incomprehensible just three to five years ago.

Corporations know that collaborative computing, using networked technologies, can provide significant competitive advantages, as well as better internal communications. The trend of downsizing has pushed the self-governing, independent employees who accomplish goals and deliverables to be more in demand. The globalization of many businesses, regardless of size, means that it is increasingly difficult to schedule face-to-face, real-time meetings. Companies have online meeting room scheduling services with speaker phones in these rooms for team members and employees to communicate from wherever they happen to be when the meeting is scheduled. The popularity of virtual teams—although many corporations do not think of these groups as virtual—and virtual corporations requires the participation from those who may not share common organizational structures; they may be alliance partners on a specific project. Groupware tools break down barriers within and between companies, affording greater efficiency, flexibility, communication, and accessibility. This only describes the communications tools for meetings; what about online tools for computer-to-computer sharing?

The collaborative software market is especially attractive to the engineering community. There is no better way for collaboration on project and documentation than a common place to put, read, and share information. Traditional productivity applications such as word processors have been available—Microsoft Word, Amipro, and Word Perfect, as well as spreadsheets, Excel, and Lotus—with minimal product differentiation. Today vendors are shifting toward more collaborative tools or adding workgroup-like features to existing software applications as a way of differentiation. Many operating-system manufacturers incorporate Netscape into their desktops, and application suite vendors—Microsoft, Lotus, and Adobe—are building collaborative functions such as group or team scheduling and group or team editing into their office or multimedia automation packages.

This world is not perfect yet, and although tools allow for better collaboration, sometimes enclosures transmitted from different companies and from one location to another appear garbled or unreadable because of various encoders and buffers found within networks. Discussions may proceed slowly via E-mail, depending on each person's schedule for reviewing new messages, and it may take time for the entire team to agree on an idea. By adding the chat and talk features of the Internet to the communications mix, another level of more instantaneous communication can be achieved globally. The current on-demand and virtual communications era requires instantaneous computer communications for business, consumers, governments, and educational institutions. The United States, in particular, has no time for delay; Americans want the information when they need it and do not tolerate delays very well. New collaborative tools overcome the instantaneous issues of distance, time, and volume barriers. It is the spirit of mass connectivity—of an increasingly wired, online world—that will and has already defined the future. The supporting information infrastructure must be prepared to meet the demands of this communications need and must encompass a wide variety of transmission issues such as bandwidth, media, and network devices, as well as a limitless array of applications and the support for all of these.

The modern executive might say that both "time and knowledge are money," as the timeliness of a product release could determine the market share and therefore the future of the corporation. Knowledge creates the money, as seen in the high demand for knowledge workers. This concept translates into highly skilled and knowledgeable workers, precise time to market, good design, understanding the demand in the marketplace, satisfying customers, just-in-time inventory control and production methods, and more profitable, visionary decision-making. And, as information flows through networks, events happen efficiently, corporations stay informed, and all of it is made possible by automated tools, well-managed networks, and highly skilled employees.

Knowledge is constantly being renewed, enhanced, and shared; it is the primary source for competitive corporate advantage. Because of this the virtual corporation must be designed to expand knowledge for all employees. The more enhanced ways employees utilize to access knowledge, the more they can contribute to corporate profits. Corporations succeed because they have greater expertise and knowledge of timing than the competition. They gather market share because they have better, more timely design, customer service, and marketing channels. Employee expertise can be amplified with computing tools, especially network-centric, LAN- and WAN-connected computing. The modern corporation supports the knowledge of all of its workers and provides them with software that enables more productivity and teamwork. The virtual corporation has a knowledge infrastructure to capture and create, store, improve, disseminate, and use knowledge for corporate advantage. Corporations in the lead constantly hold onto the competitive advantage; they are always finding ways to improve and expand their markets. The most successful companies are those that value continuous improvement and learning. Because the only way to compete is to produce faster and better than the competition, leading-edge corporations encourage experimentation on all levels in order to maintain and be better positioned for the future.

The total worldwide investment in information and communication technologies is now more than a trillion dollars per year and growing at a furious pace. The ongoing investment of technology is changing the world economy. Countries who are not in the information age will be left behind and unable to be major players in the future. The term *information economy* is often used to describe corporations that communicate and do business worldwide with real-time interactions over information superhighways and an interlaced mesh of virtual operations. Such corporations are becoming *non-national* with capital, management, talent, and resources coming from all over the world; in other words, they are becoming truly virtual in nature.

Much of a corporation's expertise and procedures are possible because of computer software. Corporate software is rapidly growing in complexity and is becoming more comprehensive and sophisticated to support the ever-changing needs of corporations. Designers of corporate operations are aware that software does not merely replicate existing operations; it also facilitates entirely different types of operations and work methodologies. Groupware has revolutionized how people work together. These groupware tools are necessary for a virtual team and virtual project to be successful and to enhance communication. Most of these collaborative groupware tools allow resources to share current information with one another easily. These applications allow for resource responses to be viewed by all team members and decision-making to be easier as a result. Often white papers are edited quickly by team members as they see one another's comments and can easily voice their opinions or add information. Applications linked via E-mail allow team members to forward copies of documents to one another within or outside the corporate bounds.

Sometimes, remote access is the best choice for communication because of the central location, content, flexibility, and availability of the documents required. Most first-generation groupware systems were closed and proprietary. The proprietary nature of these early programs, such as Lotus Notes, resulted in single-vendor architectures where it was virtually impossible to build independent applications. These were tolerated because there was a distinction between groupware applications and groupware messaging. The newest generation of groupware tools is emerging with ubiquitous application interfaces that foster inter-product compatibility. Vendors have retooled their offerings to split out the messaging and groupware applications from underlying services. One example—although not the only one—is Microsoft's Mail Application Programming Interface (MAPI). Programmers can now develop new applications using available messaging and collaborative services. The latest version of MAPI supports different vendor applications and services in a *mix and match* architecture. This openness and usability makes it possible to use one vendor's E-mail application to access messages served by another vendor's messaging server. Support for MAPI is found throughout the industry by Microsoft, Novell, Banyan, Oracle, Hewlett-Packard, and Lotus. These new interfaces are enabling more collaborative applications to be built in the future. The new generation of groupware titles on an open multivendor environment allows resources to choose the best infrastructure and applications independently.

E-mail is one of the communications tools that is vital to successful virtual project teams. Messages can be developed and sent any hour of the day or night; there is no time or distance barrier. The communication is virtually instantaneous and definitely twenty-four-hour in nature. Messages can be sent to the entire project team so that all are informed at the same time, or they may be sent to individuals. Often the project manager sets the distribution list for all team members and forwards pertinent information to the team. At times, users create and use templates as well as focused distribution lists. This is also the way that status-meeting documentation is distributed to ensure that team members have the most current and necessary materials. The project manager may use E-mail to send and receive weekly status on projects, as well. Most project planning software tools have the capability to send E-mail or Web messages concerning status. Some of them have actual timesheets for task and project status by week that is then sent to the project manager for input into a scheduling tool.

There are many shipping companies that utilize communication technology tools, as well, and may be appropriate partners for delivery. Federal Express set up a Web site for customers to find the status and location of items in shipment. This tracking capability proved extremely popular with customers and provided incentive to choose Federal Express over its competition. The company also teams with other companies to offer just-in-time shipping; items are held until they are required for delivery, thereby reducing warehouse costs for their customers.

The communication tools that the virtual team uses are important. Every member of the team must have the same basic package: laptop computer, modem, cellular phone, and pager, as well as the same or similar software suites. But there are other devices, such as cellular E-mail devices, digital pagers that receive and send E-mail, and desktop video, that could add productivity to the team. These should all be considered and evaluated as to how they could positively impact the team's productivity. First Virtual Corporation has developed one productivity tool that delivers high-quality multimedia and videoconferencing. This product is for high-speed links for images, video and audio. It does this via asynchronous mode (ATM) switches, the Internet, and ISDN gateway servers. It allows resources on the network to perform multiple videoconferencing and multimedia tasks simultaneously, without video or audio degradation. This is an important tool for virtual team communications.

The virtual team should have its first meeting face to face to better establish relationships, develop strategies, and then, if it is a long-term project, hold these face-to-face meetings every three months. If the project is of shorter duration, then the frequency of these meetings becomes less important. If the project is long, alternating videoconferencing with audio conferencing is important for variety and to present specific things to the entire group at once. These are complementary to other communications techniques already mentioned.

The term *unobtrusive accessibility*, or the idea that groupware features will fare better if integrated with features that support individual activity, suggests that collaboration or virtual teaming and other information-sharing capabilities should integrate with existing desktops and personal productivity applications. New groupware desktops, or groupware applications, are emerging that support the virtual teaming concept with greater flexibility and features than are currently available. They will become integrated into existing applications like E-mail, word processing, and graphic presentation tools and become day-to-day tools.

As ubiquitous network and Internet access reaches more of the consumer market, new categories of groupware will emerge that will become part of corporate groupware usage, as well. The social implications of a widely connected virtual community of collaborating individuals are enormous, as more opportunities for virtual teaming become more apparent. There is a caution of information overload, as is touted by many in the media, and it is fast becoming a reality. As fast as the size of the virtual community grows, the attendant traffic grows even faster. Left unchecked, groupware systems can become victims of their own success. As E-mail connectivity increases, so too does the average number of new messages appearing in the user's mailbox. The current trends indicate that many users receive fifty new messages per day; there are those who receive over 150 per day, and system administrators receive closer to 200 messages per day. Finding the time and interest to read all of these messages can become a chore in itself. There are better ways of screening messages to allow those of interest and priority to be read first, leaving the rest for leisure reading.

Improving Workflow

There is a tremendous growth in the use of E-mail and the proportionate number of messages individuals receive daily. The difficulty is determining in what order to read them. Often messages are sent just to keep the recipient informed, and they do not require any response. Other times, messages are sent that have significant deliverables attached. It is difficult to know merely by reading the subject line which message should take priority.

There are many opinions on how to prioritize messages, ranging from simply looking at the sender's name to using the functionality of the E-mail package to identify priority. This ability, if used on a project team, is very helpful in prioritizing. E-mail packages allow for sending messages with a priority, urgent, or FYI if the urgent label is used to prompt an immediate response; then at least the most critical messages will be in the forefront.

There are other vehicles for message delivery, and they all have priorities attached to them. For example, an urgent but not important message is the ringing telephone that may or may not really be an urgent call. An important but not urgent message could be that the local printer is down, and if printing is needed another printer must be used. Lastly, an urgent and important message may be that the installation is in crisis, and a decision must be made immediately.

The significance of prioritization is that more and more groupware products are on the market and in use, both confusing the project teams and cluttering up the normal workflow. The groupware market is growing dramatically and changing fundamentally, driven in part by the popularity of the Internet. The groupware deployments are changing from top-down to bottom-up and even-team deployments. Specific products may be chosen for a virtual project team to use to communicate more effectively. Groupware itself is changing from technology-centric platforms to application-focused ones, changing the way people can and need to communicate whether in a virtual project team or a virtual corporation. The trends are reshaping themselves daily and will continue to bring people together in new and more compelling ways.

Aside from computer products there are other products such as voice mail and voice messaging that are often as important for access to individuals. Of course, voice mail does not always find the person, especially if she is not at her phone. If the team member must be found, there are ways of using technologies to actually track down this person. A product called Wildfire is a personal assistant that runs on a server and directs incoming and outgoing voice communications, no matter where the user or team member is at the time. The team member supplies Wildfire with various alternate numbers for real-time access, and the technology calls each number until the team member is found. This product eliminates phone tag, the need to leave messages, and establishes a transparent connection in seconds. Team members dial an access number connecting to their own pre-programmed, computerized female-voice assistants, utilizing voice recognition technology to prompt them through the management of their incoming and outgoing calls. Wildfire can forward calls to any phone and, for example, tell hotel operators, "I'm looking for John Doe." As a good assistant it allows users to screen their calls, or it will use a pre-programmed list. If the team member is too busy to answer the call, it will send an electronic message via a digital pager, assuming that the team member is wearing the pager. Wildfire's best use is with virtual project teams; it can allow a developer, contractor, and project leader to communicate as if he was using the office voice mail system or conducting a real-time phone conversation. A virtual corporation example is CambridgeCAD Technologies, an IBM and Apple reseller, that is called upon constantly for customer support. CambridgeCAD has found that Wildfire frees employees from their desks, allowing them to answer from wherever they are. It never misses the customer and is always there to provide the support required and expected.

Workflow or process flow technologies have long been used to manage the flow of physical objects such as manufacturing parts, supplies, and documents. In the virtual corporation it often refers to the managing of electronic or information objects. The notion of information objects is critical to understanding workflow or any other virtual process. An information object is the electronic representation of something such as a component, product, service package, or document. It may be a precursor or prototype to the actual product, such as a CAD drawing of a design, representing the advanced state of the object in the design, or an online report that will eventually become a printed report. It also may be the object itself, something electronic that will never be a physical product, such as E-mail messages, minutes from a meeting, an online magazine, or a research database. Workflow moves information objects from one position or station to another, person to person, through a network. This can be as simple as routing a travel reimbursement through the required approval process to tracking where each component for a system is at any given time in the manufacture of the space shuttle, for example.

Behind the use of these technologies is a key belief in virtual work, that is, of keeping all output such as products and services electronically, for as long as possible in the life cycle. Electronic representations are more flexible and accessible, and they provide the ability to capture multiple perspectives, increase validity, and often reduce overhead. Workflow is often used as an automation technology for streamlining existing processes and procedures. The same workflow process is needed for document routing, such as travel approval and information routing.

A large, multistate bank recently conducted a workflow study in its retail loan department. The bank was acquiring a document imaging system that would change the way it processed loans; therefore, it needed to document and baseline its existing workflow processes. Company employees found that they were able to complete twenty loans a week using their paper workflow, which stopped at various desks on its way to being approved. After implementing the new technology, conducting training, and providing laptop computers to their field sales force, employees started to watch the new workflow, noting the results of the change. After the implementation and training, they found that sales people in the field were sending in loan applications, and the department was able to process twenty loans per day, thereby increasing their revenues significantly. Consequently, they moved from the paper workflow to an online workflow process as a standard.

In the airline business, software fundamentally changed the booking process worldwide and made it possible to have many prices for the same seat so that revenue from the flight could be maximized. When American Airlines was highly profitable, the chief executive officer was asked if he would ever consider selling the airline. He replied: "Given the choice of selling the airline or selling its software, SABRE, I would rather sell the airline, as the software is more valuable." Of course, he had no intention of selling American Airlines, but at the time, SABRE was more profitable and required far less maintenance then the airlines. European airlines are using competitive products, such as AMADEUS and GALILEO, and are struggling to combat the effects of SABRE moving into Europe. May the best software win!

A Software Development Virtual Team Project

The explosive growth in global networking infrastructures managed by telecommunications companies has begun opening new possibilities for global collaborative processes. One of the benefits of the proper use of global networking is software development. It is feasible for virtual teams of software developers to be assembled intelligently and swiftly on a project basis from a global pool of resources. The project owner is able to manage the development process using workflow technologies that can be deployed over a global network such as the Internet. Developers and testers can be equipped with development environments, tools, and methodologies that are logical extensions of their current environments and practices. A suitable team communication infrastructure can be put in place to facilitate unstructured communication between team members.

It appears universal that managing large software development efforts is difficult. The most troublesome areas have to do with the economics of planning and the actual execution. This issue can benefit greatly by utilizing the Internet and other global networks for global dissemination of information. Currently, co-located teams and traditional project management are often plagued with logistical problems such as identifying and assembling skilled teams, timely procurement of supporting products and services, and the optimal work breakdown of the project into manageable pieces. Project execution almost always suffers from scope, schedule, and cost creep. Tracking the progress of a project and recovering from schedule discrepancies and disruptions are often ad hoc activities at best. Often in these cases the project manager is a member of the design team and therefore responsible for deliverables as well as for managing and controlling the project. Virtual project management radically changes the way that teams are constructed and projects are conducted. It aims toward altering the economics of providing large-scale services and significantly improving the efficiency of implementing large projects.

The concept of virtual service providers and virtual project teams participating in the planning and execution of large software development efforts over the Internet and other global networks is key. It begins with the premise that a software development project is planned and executed by a number of virtual teams or virtual service providers. These participants communicate via the Internet and global networks, which act as virtual delivery mechanisms. Utilization of the Internet has been an effective medium for many applications and projects. The most prominent and heavily used ones are E-mail, News, FTP, Telnet, the WWW, and IRC. The emergence of Java and other related scripting languages, and their endorsements by the Internet community, indicates that executable, downloadable content will soon become commonplace and a mainstream feature on the Web. The two most promising developments from the point of view of Internet users will be interactivity and animation. This could mean that users would interact with live content on the Web and thereby could affect the actual behavior of the content. This is a transformation of the Web from a global, static, publication medium to a global, interactive, real-time, software execution environment that will enable completely new developments for software applications.

Primarily, the potential of utilizing the Internet as a viable networking medium for distributed, wide-area software applications is becoming increasingly attractive. This is possible because the Internet can provide so much in terms of sharing, teaming, and collaboration. It could provide an ubiquitous client-server platform for software applications and a global programming infrastructure for software development efforts that could run on any machine connected to the Internet. The global execution environment for software applications may provide a tremendous opportunity for collaboration. It could evolve into wide-area networking, structured or unstructured collaboration among dispersed people, structured or unstructured collaboration across organizational and country boundaries, and access to human or computer resources on a global scale.

While the key to virtual operations is connectivity and integration, the possibilities for disintegration are great. For example, left to their own devices, individual departments tend to design their own data and select their own software. This mess of incompatibility could spread so that future change would require conversion efforts that are often slow, painful, and expensive. Flexible connectivity requires common data and objects, rather than the same data and objects having different representations in different systems. Virtual operation needs structured planning with a strategic look to the future instead of stove-piped departments doing their own tactical things. The virtual corporation view has a large payoff and raises vital questions about the enterprise's overall architecture and information technologies. It raises questions about when business reengineering is a good idea, for example. Most managers in most corporations confine their thinking to their own areas and their daily operations, while the virtual corporation should be conceived in terms of end-to-end activities and connectivity that often spans multiple departments, divisions, and maybe even corporations.

The Internet and its evolving structure holds great promise for becoming an attractive infrastructure for large software development efforts in the future. In place of a traditional software development co-located team, a virtual team can be assembled from a global resource pool. Imagine the possibilities if skilled resources were registered in a common database, and the project manager could draw from the pool when a certain type of resource was required. Of course there would be interviews, via the Internet, to ensure that the resources fit the exact work required and that the resources were both available and not overloaded. Communications, reporting, and workflow strategies would be agreed upon once the team was assembled and an initial meeting held via a *chat session* on the Internet. A software development process could then be initiated utilizing a server owned by the project owner. These dispersed virtual team members would receive their work assignments from the server and interact with their respective clients over the Internet. The project manager would be responsible for team status and reporting through the Internet, and the actual workflow would guide the development process through the various stages until the project was completed. Along the way there would be review sessions with the project owner but, depending on the owner's experience and comfort with the Internet, these meetings could also be conducted online or in a videoconference.

There are many challenging technical and social aspects of this concept. The promise of becoming an attractive infrastructure for large software development projects is quite compelling. Software development is a complex process even when efforts are concentrated in one location; dispersing the team members adds far greater complexity than necessary, it seems. The up-front planning and both communication and reporting strategies are critical if this concept is to be a success. It is true that engineers work alone and in very intense fashions during their efforts, so logistics should really become unimportant. The issue has to do with controlling the output, which is always important. In addition, there is a tremendous amount of data gathering and database input to have quality information for virtual use. There must be someone responsible for the accuracy and integrity of the database information so that when resources are taken for projects, for example, this is reflected in the database as unavailability. It is clear, though, that economic benefits far outweigh the drawbacks of this unique idea.

The emerging software development marketplace is beginning to show certain interesting characteristics. For example, the software resource pool is, in fact, quite global. Contract development companies, programmers, designers, testers, and maintainers are available in different parts of the world today, often aligned with companies in the United States. Also, the quality of software development infrastructure in different parts of the world may be comparable and, then again, may not be. Operating systems such as Unix, Windows 95, OS/2, and Windows NT are universal. The relational databases, such as Oracle, DB2, Sybase, and Informix are ubiquitous, as well. Development tools such as Visual Basic, Visual C++, Xmotif, and PowerBuilder are also commonly used. Complex software products often involve one-time processes that require participants with specialized talents and skills for the duration of the project. Contracting the best and most talented resources for a project is a viable option when hiring is not. Emerging global delivery systems and infrastructures for electronic mail, file transfer, remote login, and the Web are available throughout the world as more and more countries open their networks to the Internet.

In summary, virtual software development teams can offer many unique advantages over traditional teams. For example, they provide a global resource pool of talented engineers, programmers, designers, testers, and maintainers, thus providing an effective resource and skill utilization, a phenomenon common to corporations operating from multiple sites. These teams can incrementally reduce costs, eliminate major travel, and, consequently, lost time while traveling, and reduce related overhead associated with a locally located team.

Assembling a Virtual, Distributed Project Team: A Prototype

An observation can be made to an outsider that the process of assembling a virtual project team is very much like organizing a National Basketball Association (NBA) or National Football League (NFL) team. The project (franchise) owner plays a key role in assembling the virtual (NBA or NFL) project team. Once the project scope has been documented, the project owner must consider who will be project manager (coach), and who will staff the project, otherwise known as the skilled resources (players). One scenario might be as follows.

The project (franchise) owner has worked with various software development project managers (coaches) in the past and solicits assistance from them. Depending on the scope of the project and availability of the project manager, one is chosen that would be a strong, knowledgeable, and appropriate project manager to lead this effort. The project owner, with the assistance of the project manager, announces a software project with the project description and notifies *interested parties* (players) via focused E-mail, newsgroups, or mailing list broadcasts. This notification directs interested parties to contact an Internet site for the project. Interested parties visit the project site and gather information and perhaps ask questions, then bid on parts of the project (negotiate terms) for which they have skills or resources within their development companies having the required skill sets. In order to bid, downloadable forms provided by the project owner have to be completed for estimating and budgeting time and costs and to ensure consistency between bids. The forms (contracts) are then completed by a specific date and forwarded to the project owner for review and evaluation. The project owner, with assistance from the project manager, evaluates the bids and notifies bidders of acceptance or rejection. Successful bidders are then invited to join the virtual project team.

Challenges for the project owner include the need for a reliable, comprehensive locator service like the yellow pages on the Internet, developing the comprehensive bid packages for the electronic marketplace, and then evaluating responses. This could be a logistics nightmare, depending on the volume of bids submitted; perhaps automated evaluation criteria could be designed to assist in the effort. The checking of credentials to verify the bidder's information and to check past work habits would be the last step.

Is this really a dream, or could setting up a virtual project team via the Internet be possible in the future? Today, jobs are advertised online and resumes can be forwarded; only the truly viable candidates are interviewed. This concept is not really that far-fetched based on how the Internet and its uses are developing.

Managing the Virtual Project Team

Once the members of the virtual project team are identified, the actual project planning effort begins with developing a project plan and workflow model that represents the integrated, multiorganizational project. A typical scenario might be as follows. The project manager defines or refines the software development project plan and workflow models, which also involves developing tasks and their dependencies. These dependencies will include design, prototype, implement, unit test, build, integration testing, and so on, as well as roles and responsibilities for the task owner, subcontractors, designers, programmers, testers, and maintainers. Also, tools associated with tasks and roles, such as project management tools, configuration and management tools, programming and testing environments, and so forth should be included.

The next step would involve implementing a software development project workflow that is located on an Internet-enabling workflow server. At this point, a methodology is established for ensuring that the logical progression of work occurs among the multiple participants, and it should be a methodology that can be modified and visualized using tools provided by the owner and used by the project manager and participants.

There are key technical issues involved in this enterprise, as well. For example, the Internet will serve as the networking backbone for the transfer of work items, project parts, and results between participating organizations. Of course, this assumes that the project owner has contracted with an agency instead of with individuals. The workflow model used must be rich and flexible enough to support the concept of multiple participating organizations, during which each organization selectively offers its key resources and internals to its project partners. This introduces the concept of privacy and intellectual property, as well as competition, and again assumes that the project owner has contracted with an agency instead of with individuals. When a part of the project, sub-project, or sub-workflow is assigned to a participating organization, it is the responsibility of the participating organization to assign its own resources to the project tasks. The project owner and project manager do not have any control over specific assignments as long as they conform to the project constraints.

It may not be feasible to expect multiple-participant organizations to use the same set of tools and environments; therefore, each participant may utilize local tools and environments. The project and workflow management systems will be distributive in nature, with each participant organization running its own workflow server that can execute workflows downloaded to it; the project server will be able to coordinate with the participant's servers. Heterogeneous workflow servers will necessitate interoperability among servers. Some design characteristics of the workflow protocol should include participants having a view of the development process and their roles in it. A push or pull from the workflow server updates this view. In some project management tools, the application will send a timesheet with tasks required of the participant for that specific week and allow the participant to send the updates directly to the project manager of the project plan. Another characteristic of the workflow protocol would be allowing the project workflow server to initiate, suspend, abort, resume, and deal with other exceptions that are transmitted to the participant's workflow server for the appropriate action.

Environments and Protocols. Every participant's user interface includes an environment, which is a toolkit or workbench allowing participants to perform their tasks. Environments are role specific. For example, a project owner's environment consists of tools suitable for project management to enable estimating, planning, and budgeting. A project owner's environment would include project site management tools, workflow design, and coordination and monitoring tools, as well as project management tools, and the project participant's environment would consist of workflow coordination, monitoring tools, and project management tools. Other examples are the software developer's environment, consisting of editing, workflow client, libraries, compilers, debuggers, analysis tools, visualization tools, and configuration management tools, and the software tester's environment, consisting of editing, workflow client, test case generators, and configuration management systems. The software designer's environment would comprise editing, workflow client, design, and visualization tools.

While many tools may be local to the participant, it may be advantageous in the context of the Internet to centralize certain tools and environments. For example, shared software artifacts can be maintained in a server-side repository accessible over the Internet through the project site Web server and a gateway. This can work for shared resources, such as a configuration management system, search tools, and code query processors. The shared artifacts of interest may include specifications, design documents, codes, versions, documents, test cases, bug reports, and other relevant information.

Team Communications. Workflow systems handle the structured aspects of business processes. Critical to the success of the team's project is maintaining a forum for unstructured and semi-structured communications and reporting methodologies. A well-established infrastructure for team communications is absolutely essential to the success of a virtual project team. The social hurdles of enabling virtual teams may very well outnumber the technical challenges, although this is not to say that the technical challenges are inconsequential. Existing technologies that are often used for such communications and reporting in virtual project management include E-mail, mailing and distribution lists, newsgroups, discussion forums, faxes, and audio conferencing and videoconferencing. Above all else, a sense of flexibility and accountability must be nurtured and maintained.

In the near future, it may be desirable to include collaborative activities as integral components of workflow systems. Workflow systems offering native support for co-located and distributed synchronous and asynchronous collaboration among groups may be indispensable, if not an absolute requirement. As these concepts are in their development stages, it is too early to say if they will actually come to pass, as suggested here. The general concept of virtual project management is quite attractive in its economic implications, resource opportunities, globalization, and distributed and technological opportunities and innovations.

Entering the 21st Century: Virtual Companies

Verifone is a $260 million credit card verification company headquartered in Redwood City, California, in the United States (U.S.). It began operations in 1982 as a virtual corporation and has grown from five employees to 2,500 in fourteen years. Verifone prides itself on its communications strategies, having used communications and information technology tools from the beginning. It was necessary to provide access because many of their executives are located in Redwood City and Los Angeles, California, and Sante Fe, New Mexico (U.S.), and expressed no desire to relocate.

Verifone accepted the communications challenge: changing deeply entrenched workplace habits. One way to accomplish this was by changing the primary meeting place from the office to the computer network. There is a new way of expecting to see information; it must be on the network because the work force is so dispersed. Verifone does conduct face-to-face meetings every six weeks to ensure that the teams are functioning well and to rekindle relationships, but generally the company has a corporate culture that embraces computers and online information. The face-to-face meetings support the corporate culture. One way to ensure that the online information is valid is to constantly update the financial databases for company-wide sales information. This is critical as the enterprise must be able to view real-time information whenever necessary.

Another innovation is that Verifone will approve the purchase of capital equipment expenditures online, thereby eliminating paperwork and delays due to staff illness or omission. Once the expenditure is approved, the staff can search the negotiated vendor list to purchase with the corporate discounts. E-mail—one of the primary communications techniques used to share information—is used to clarify, ask questions, share specific documents, and understand the business growth through conversations and chat sessions.

Verifone is a true example of a virtual global enterprise; its teams are virtual project teams with members distributed across the globe. There are developers in Dallas, Texas, in the U.S., that send unfinished work to Laupahoehoe, Hawaii, for input. It is sent from there to Bangalore, India, and then back to Dallas, sixteen hours closer to completion. Verifone is a twenty-four-hour operation that utilizes its infrastructure network to assist in the completion of projects. The company is based on the idea that tasks need to be automate tasks that do not waste people's time. If people are more productive, their sense of accomplishment and self-esteem will rise accordingly. Verifone automates for morale, as well as for productivity.

Verifone uses over sixty different computer-based applications for online processing. Many are tested, and those that truly deliver to expectations and results are implemented company-wide. For example, Verifone has created a company-wide electronic filing cabinet that is available to all employees and business partners. Its E-mail, correspondence, reports, and forms are filed online, effectively eliminating lost documents, and it utilizes electronic time stamping in order to know when documents have been received. This also allows remote access to contracts, forms, files, and reports. There are computerized order entry and accounting databases, as well as best practice files and project information, for reuse at other times.

Verifone has made its systems easy to use and navigate, thereby supporting a more productive environment. The virtual teams often are informal teams with E-mail group aliases and audio conferencing and videoconferencing capability. All employees are given access to these technologies and use them when necessary. There is quite a bit of flexibility in quickly forming and dissolving teams as needed, enhancing the virtual team concept at its best.

In late 1994 Federal Express had an idea; the company created a Web site to allow customers the ability to track their packages online. Previously unheard of, this concept gave Federal Express customers autonomy and, at the same time, freed company employees from addressing these requests. It even gives customers the ability to see if there are problems before Federal Express is aware of them, in some instances. Today nearly 12,000 customers use this service and consider it a necessary and valuable tool, and Federal Express has saved over $2 million per year by offering the service. Whenever a new customer signs with the company, he is asked if he would like the software to track his own packages and, if so, what platform he uses. Customers are given the software at the same time they receive their customer numbers. It is an innovative way to use embedded systems.

Federal Express is currently establishing sixty sites for their employees, who will soon have Web browsers to access sites for additional information. Intranets make it easier to find company information wherever it is located. Federal Express has realized that more access to information allows their employees to feel a strong connection to the company while being more productive.

Rickard Associates, a magazine producer with offices throughout the U.S., has a virtual project team that includes an Arizona art director and editors in Florida, Georgia, Michigan, and the District of Columbia. The company uses America Online for E-mail, article editing, and review. America Online was chosen because Rickard wanted to have the same E-mail system and provider to be able to send and receive enclosures without the problems associated with dissimilar E-mail packages. Its Navistar International system allows the team to have remote access to over 600 locations in North America. Rickard also relies heavily on its electronic network for sharing information and communications. The virtual project team is a reality for Rickard and it continues to use this concept in developing materials.

Tower Concepts of New York (U.S.) uses the Internet to market, deliver, and update its computer programming software. Compaq Computer, a virtual corporation, allows its employees around the world to tap into a Web server to reallocate investments in their 401(k) plans. Apollo Travel uses frame relay to distribute computer reservations data to 15,000 virtual U.S. travel agents. Ford Motor Co., via its wide area network infrastructure, linked its virtual design centers in Asia, Europe, and the U.S. for the 1996 Ford Taurus design and planning. This virtual team concept was so successful that what was once an experiment is now the model for the way cars are designed and manufactured worldwide by Ford.

National Semiconductor allows employees to create home pages for department meeting scheduling. Prudential Insurance Co., a virtual company spread across the U.S., is upgrading its network to include ATM and frame relay for image and resource sharing nationwide. Monsanto, a U.S.-based virtual corporation, is currently testing a simultaneous computer-based document sharing technology for its distributed work force. Silicon Graphics, another virtual corporation with offices around the world, has 7,200 employees with access to its 144,000 Web pages stored on its internal Web sites. The company provides its worldwide virtual project teams with computers with video cameras to allow for communication and video-conferencing.

These are only a few examples to illustrate that virtual project management provides a leading edge in this new wave of the future.

And in the End

There really is no end to what can be done with the addition of technology to projects or operations. Everyday new capabilities are being introduced that will allow better, faster, and easier access to information. Searching the net for information about competitors is easy.

Setting up repositories for virtual teams outside the corporate firewall is now offered. This capability allows for resources from different companies to share common information without the security scare of allowing network access. This is a service that can be subscribed to with password protection so that the team can share documents, hold chat sessions, have a common bulletin board, and generally electronically communicate globally.

The ability to have one phone number follow you around the world is being tested with satellites, as we speak, and will seem like old news before long. Remote access to networks and Internet service providers (ISPs) does not even require physical connectivity; it can be accomplished via cellular and digital networks.

As the technology capability and availability increases, the benefits to virtual project teams and virtual operations will increase, as well. The trends now indicate that more and more people will be working from remote locations, telecommuting or not having dedicated office space at all. Today's children, college students, and recent graduates expect the technology to enable them more work freedom. They are growing up with the Internet and computers; companies who want to stay competitive will need to have transitioned to virtual operations in order to compete for these workers.

Time is of the essence for companies to wake up and realize that they cannot wait any longer to begin this transition. If the trend is not started at the top, then workers will start their own virtual operations and seek corporations who value this work style. Computers and technology have and will continue to change and fashion the way we work and communicate.

Pay attention to the corporations in the news, the corporations that are leading the pack with their use and applications of technologies. Begin to notice how you are using more and more technology and expecting certain service levels from your service providers. Things are speeding up whether we like it or not, and virtual corporations and virtual operations are pointing the way. Virtual applications will continue to allow access to information. Computers with global mapping in cars facilitate finding locations. Kiosks on streets will allow for finding businesses in the area. Global news teams will continue to bring world news into our homes.

How many news services or newsletters do you get electronically at present? How do you receive information today? Will you receive it in the same way tomorrow?

The virtual edge will separate the leaders from the followers. Ask yourself which position you want to be in: leader or follower? Dare to step over the edge.

References

Berk, Robert. 1996. *Virtual Teaming* (Mar.).

Chaar, Jarr, Paul Santanu, and Ram Chillarege. 1996. Virtual Project Management Software Workflow Application and Services. NSF Workshop on Workflow & Process Automation (May).

Grenier, Ray, and George Metes. 1992. *Enterprise Networking: Working Together Apart*. Maynard, Massachusetts: Digital Press.

————. 1995. *Going Virtual*. New Jersey: Prentice Hall.

A Guide to the Project Management Body of Knowledge (PMBOK Guide). 1996. Drexel Hall, Pennsylvania: Project Management Institute.

Juned, S. 1996. Team Based European Automotive Manufacturing Inter-project Links and Delivery Chains. Available on the Internet.

Mall, Kathleen, and Sirdka Jarvenpaa. 1995. Learning to Work in Distributed Global Teams. HICSS. Available from www.uts.cc.utexas.edu/bgac313/hicss.html on the Internet.

Kostner, Jaclyn. 1996. *Virtual Leadership*. New York: Warner Books.

Leonard-Barton, Dorothy, Justine Fenwick, Marolyn Matis, Paul Brands, and Daniel Schriebman. 1995. *Managing Geographically Dispersed Teams*. Harvard Business School: American Management NYU.

Naisbett J., and P. Abardene. 1990. *Megatrends 2000: Ten New Directions for the 1990s*. New York: Morrow.

Necroponte, Nicholas. 1995. *Being Digital*. London: Hodder & Stoughton.

Schroeder, Erica, and Paula Musich. 1995. First Virtual Puts Multimedia over ATM. *Progress Software*.

Teams in the 21st Century Newsletter. 1996. MSI (Dec.).

Vonder Haar, Steven. 1996. WalMart Plans Online Expansion. *ZDNet News* (Dec.).

PMI's Tools for Training

A Guide to the Project Management Body of Knowledge

The basic management reference for everyone who works on projects. Serves as a tool for learning about the generally accepted knowledge and practices of the profession. As "management by projects" becomes more and more a recommended business practice worldwide, the *PMBOK Guide* becomes an essential source of information that should be on every manager's bookshelf. Available in hardcover or paperback, the *PMBOK Guide* is an official standards document of the Project Management Institute.

ISBN: 1-880410-12-5 (paperback), 1-880410-13-3 (hardcover)

Interactive PMBOK Guide

This CD-ROM makes it easy for you to access the valuable information in PMI's *A Guide to the Project Management Body of Knowledge*. Features hypertext links for easy reference—simply click on underlined works in the text, and the software will take you to that particular section in the *PMBOK Guide*. Minimum system requirements: 486 PC, 8MB RAM, 10MB free disk space, CD-ROM drive, mouse or other pointing device, and Windows 3.1 or greater.

PMBOK Review Package

This "Box of Books" offers you a set of materials that supplements the *PMBOK Guide* in helping you develop a deeper understanding of the Project Management Body of Knowledge and helps you prepare for the PMP® certification exam. These important and authoritative publications offer the depth and breadth you need to learn more about all the *PMBOK Guide* knowledge areas. Includes the following titles: *Project Management: A Managerial Approach; Project Planning, Scheduling & Control; Human Resource Skills for the Project Manager; Project and Program Risk Management; Quality Management for Projects & Programs; PMBOK Q&A; Managing the Project Team; Organizing Projects for Success;* and *Principles of Project Management.*

Managing Projects Step-by-Step™

Follow the steps, standards, and procedures used and proven by thousands of professional project managers and leading corporations. This interactive multimedia CD-ROM based on PMI's *A Guide to the Project Management Body of Knowledge* will enable you to customize, standardize, and distribute your project plan standards, procedures, and methodology across your entire organization. Multimedia illustrations using 3-D animations and audio make this perfect for both self-paced training or for use by a facilitator.

PMBOK Q&A

Use this handy pocket-sized question-and-answer study guide to learn more about the key themes and concepts presented in PMI's international standard, *A Guide to the Project Management Body of Knowledge*. More than 160 multiple-choice questions with answers (referenced to the *PMBOK Guide*) help you with the breadth of knowledge needed to understand key project management concepts.
ISBN: 1-880410-21-4

Project Management Casebook

Most project managers would agree that the best way to learn new concepts and techniques is to practice them as you learn them. The case study approach has proven to be an effective way to demonstrate the practical applications of project management theory, and the case studies presented in this book show you how and why projects are used in a wide variety of organizational settings in contemporary life. Fifty cases are categorized by one of the following areas: planning, organizing, motivating, directing, controlling, and general.
Edited by David Cleland, Karen Bursic, Richard Puerzer, and A. Yaroslav Vlasak
ISBN: 1-880410-45-1

Project Management Casebook Instructor's Manual

A companion to the *Project Management Casebook*, this *Instructor's Manual* presents discussion and possible answers for each of the questions posed in the *Casebook*.
Edited by David Cleland, Karen Bursic, Richard Puerzer, and A. Yaroslav Vlasak
ISBN: 1-880410-18-4

PMI Proceedings Library CD-ROM

This interactive guide to PMI's Annual Seminars & Symposium Proceedings offers a powerful new option to the traditional methods of document storage and retrieval, research, training, and technical writing. Contains complete paper presentations from PMI '91–PMI '97. Full text search capability, convenient on-screen readability, and PC/Mac compatibility.

PMI Publications Library CD-ROM

Using state-of-the-art technology, PMI offers complete articles and information from its major publications on one CD-ROM, including *PM Network* (1991–97), *Project Management Journal* (1991–97), and *A Guide to the Project Management Body of Knowledge*. Offers full text search capability and indexing by *PMBOK Guide* knowledge areas. Electronic indexing schemes and sophisticated search engines help to find and retrieve articles quickly that are relevant to your topic or research area.

PMI Book of Project Management Forms

More than 150 actual samples and documents, used daily in the management of projects, have been compiled for you to adapt or expand upon. PMI members share forms, checklists, reports, charts, and other sample documents they use in managing their projects to make it easy for practicing project managers or students to get started or to improve their documentation. Spiral bound or CD-ROM formats available.

ISBN: 1-880410-31-1

Also Available from PMI

Principles of Project Management
John Adams et al.
ISBN: 1-880410-30-3

Organizing Projects for Success
Human Aspects of Project Management Series, Volume 1
Vijay Verma
ISBN: 1-880410-40-0

Human Resource Skills for the Project Manager
Human Aspects of Project Management Series, Volume 2
Vijay Verma
ISBN: 1-880410-41-9

Managing the Project Team
Human Aspects of Project Management Series, Volume 3
Vijay Verma
ISBN: 1-880410-42-7

Earned Value Project Management
Quentin Fleming, Joel Koppelman
ISBN: 1-880410-38-9

Value Management Practice
Michel Thiry
ISBN: 1-880410-14-1

Decision Analysis in Projects
John Schuyler
ISBN: 1-880410-39-7

ABCs of DPC
PMI's Design-Procurement-Construction Specific Interest Group
ISBN: 1-880410-07-9

The World's Greatest Project
Russell Darnall
ISBN: 1-880410-46-X

Power & Politics in Project Management
Jeffrey Pinto
ISBN: 1-880410-43-5

Best Practices of Project Management Groups in Large Functional Organizations
Frank Toney, Ray Powers
ISBN: 1-880410-05-2

Project Management in Russia
Vladimir I. Voropajev
ISBN: 1-880410-02-8

Experience, Cooperation and the Future:
The Global Status fo Project Management Profession
ISBN: 1-880410-04-4

A Framework for Project and Program Management Integration
R. Max Wideman
ISBN: 1-880410-01-X

Quality Management for Projects & Programs
Lewis R. Ireland
ISBN: 1-880410-11-7

Project & Program Risk Management
R. Max Wideman
ISBN: 1-880410-06-0

Send orders to:

PMI Headquarters
Four Campus Boulevard
Newtown Square, Pennsylvania 19073-3299 USA

Or call 610-356-4600 or fax 610-356-4647

Order online at www.pmibookstore.org